STUDIES IN ITALIAN RENAISSANCE ARCHITECTURE

Wolfgang Lotz

STUDIES IN
ITALIAN RENAISSANCE
ARCHITECTURE

Editorial Committee:
James S. Ackerman, W. Chandler Kirwin, Henry A. Millon.

Translators:
Margaret Breitenbach, Renate Franciscono, Paul Lunde.

STUDIES IN
ITALIAN RENAISSANCE
ARCHITECTURE

Wolfgang Lotz

WITHDRAWN

The MIT Press
Cambridge, Massachusetts,
and London, England

Third printing, 1987

This book was published with the assistance of the Graham Foundation for Advanced Studies in the Fine Arts.
First MIT Press paperback edition, 1981
Copyright © 1977 by
The Massachusetts Institute of Technology

This book was set in Linotype Garamond by Bi-Comp, Incorporated, printed and bound by Murray Printing Company in the United States of America.

Library of Congress Cataloging in Publication Data

Lotz, Wolfgang, 1912–
    Studies in Italian Renaissance architecture.

    Includes bibliographies and index.
    1. Architecture, Renaissance—Italy—Addresses, essays, lectures. 2. Architecture—Italy—Addresses, essays, lectures. I. Title.
NA1115.L67   720'.945   76–44833
ISBN 0–262–12073–9 (hard)
        0–262–62036–7 (paper)

CONTENTS

PREFACE

The publication of this book would not have been possible without the generosity of the Graham Foundation for Advanced Studies in the Fine Arts. I am extremely grateful for this help.

I am not entirely sure whether my friends James S. Ackerman and Henry A. Millon should be praised or blamed for encouraging me to embark on the enterprise of republishing these essays; in any event my warmest thanks go to them. It would be difficult, however, to acknowledge sufficiently James Ackerman's kindness in writing the introduction. Coming from him, it gives luster to the book. He also lent his formidable talents to the ungrateful task of translation: his work on the article on Vigevano makes that study better than I feel it is. By the same token, I wish to thank Kathleen Weil-Garris for her kind and tireless assistance in heightening the precision and readability of the entire series of essays. Finally, I owe thanks to Margaret Breitenbach, Renate Franciscono, and Paul Lunde, who were responsible for the translations from German and Italian. Chandler Kirwin took upon himself the unending work of the editing of the book.

I have added brief postscripts to the essays which refer to important publications that have appeared since mine, thereby pointing to current scholarship on the problems discussed.

Wolfgang Lotz
Rome
Bibliotheca Hertziana
(Max-Planck-Institut)
December 1975

BIBLIOGRAPHY
1938–1974
WOLFGANG LOTZ

1938 *Vignola-Studien.* Würzburg.

1938 "Vignola-Zeichnungen." *Jahrbuch der Preussischen Kunstsammlungen* 59: pp. 97–115.

1938 Review of R. Salvini, *Michele Pacher, in Zeitschrift für Kunstgeschichte* 7: pp. 92–93

1940 "Eine Deinokrates-Darstellung des Francesco di Giorgio." *Mitteilungen des Kunsthistorischen Instituts in Florenz* 5: pp. 428–433.

1940 "Entwürfe Sangallos und Peruzzis für S. Giacomo in Augusta." *Mitteilungen des Kunsthistorischen Instituts in Florenz* 5: pp. 441–444.

1940 "Italienische Baukunst des Cinquecento." *Zeitschrift für Kunstgeschichte* 9: pp. 224–230.

1940 "Michelozzos Umbau der SS. Annunziata in Florenz." *Mitteilungen des Kunsthistorischen Instituts in Florenz* 5: pp. 402–422.

1940 Review of E. Langenskjoeld, *Michele Sanmicheli, in Zeitschrift für Kunstgeschichte* 9: pp. 216–220.

1940 Review of H. Pée, *Andrea Palladios Palastbauten, in Zeitschrift für Kunstgeschichte* 9: pp. 216–220.

1940–"Die Michaels-Statue des
1941 Aegidius von Wiener Neustadt in Montemerlo." *Jahresberichte des Kunsthistorischen Instituts in Florenz.* Appendix.

1941 Review of J. Lauts, *Antonello da Messina*, in *La Rinascita* 4: pp. 292–293.

1941 Review of L. Planiscig, *Lorenzo Ghiberti*, in *La Rinascita* 4: pp. 289–291.

1942 "Due leggii inglesi nella chiesa della SS. Annunziata." *Rivista d'Arte* 24: pp. 49–59.

1942 Review of C. Cottafavi, *Il Palazzo Ducale di Mantova*, in *Zeitschrift für Kunstgeschichte* 10: pp. 228–229.

1942 Review of E. Rigoni, *Andrea Moroni*, in *Zeitschrift für Kunstgeschichte* 10: pp. 227–228.

1948 *Der Taufbrunnen des Baptisteriums zu Siena*, "Der Kunstbrief," no. 50. Berlin.

1948 "Florentiner Notizen." *Kunstchronik* 1, nos. 7/8: pp. 5–7.

1949 "Ausstellung zeitgenössischer Plastik." *Die Kunst und das Schöne Heim* 47: pp. 130–133.

1949 "Fragen des Wiederaufbaus in München: Die Residenz." *Kunstchronik* 2: pp. 165–169.

1949 Review of C. Baroni, *L'Architettura Lombarda al Bramante al Richini*, in *Zeitschrift für Kunstgeschichte* 12: pp. 108–112.

1949 Review of "From the National Gallery Laboratory," in *Kunstchronik* 2: p. 52.

1949 Review of F. Kimball, *The Creation of the Rococo*, in *Kunstchronik* 2: pp. 68–71.

1950 Review of P. B. Coremans, *Van Megeren's Faked Vermeers*, in *Kunstchronik* 3: pp. 95–96.

1951 "Antonio Gentili or Manno Sbarri." *The Art Bulletin* 33: pp. 260–262.

1952 Chapter on "The Italian and German Renaissance." *Plan und Bauwerk*. Exhibition, Munich.

1952 "Zum Problem des Karolingischen Westwerks." *Kunstchronik* 5: pp. 65–71.

1953 "Historismus in der Grabplastik um 1600: Bemerkungen zu einigen Grabmälern des Bamberger Domes." *Anzeiger des Germanischen Nationalmuseums*. pp. 61–86.

1953 Review of R. Pane. *Andrea Palladio*, in *Zeitschrift für Kunstgeschichte* 16: pp. 77–78.

1955 *The Northern Renaissance*. Art Treasures of the World. New York.

1955 "Die ovalen Kirchenräume des Cinquecento. *Römisches Jahrbuch für Kunstgeschichte* 7: pp. 7–99.

1955 Review of W. Braunfels, *Mittelalterliche Stadtbaukunst in der Toskana*, in *The Art Bulletin* 27: pp. 64–67.

1956 "Das Raumbild in der Architekturzeichnung der italienischen Renaissance." *Mitteilungen des Kunsthistorischen Instituts in Florenz* 7: pp. 193–226.

1958 "Architecture in the Later Sixteenth Century." *College Art Journal* 17, no. 2: pp. 129–139.

1958 Review of James S. Ackerman, *The Cortile of the Belvedere*, in *Kunstchronik* 11: pp. 96–100.

1961 "L'Eredità Romana di Jacopo Sansovino Architetto Veneziano." *Bollettino del Centro Internazionale di Studi di Architettura 'Andrea Palladio'* 3: pp. 82–85.

1961 "Zu Hermann Vischers d. J. Aufnahmen italienischer Bauten." *Miscellanea Bibliothecæ Hertzianæ.* pp. 167–174.

1962 "Osservazioni intorno ai disegni Palladiani." *Bollettino del Centro Internazionale di Studi di Architettura 'Andrea Palladio'.* 4: pp. 61–68.

1962 "La Rotonda: Edificio civile con cupola." *Bollettino del Centro Internazionale di Studi di Architettura 'Andrea Palladio'.* 4: pp. 69–73.

1963 "Mannerism in Architecture: Changing Aspects." *Studies in Western Art, 2: The Renaissance and Mannerism. Acts of the Twentieth International Congress of the History of Art.* pp. 239–246. Princeton, N.J.

1963 "Raffaels Sixtinische Madonna im Urteil der Kunstgeschichte." *Jahrbuch 1963 der Max-Planck-Gesellschaft zur Förderung der Wissenschaften e V.* pp. 118–128.

1963 "The Roman Legacy in Jacopo Sansovino's Venetian Buildings." *Journal of the Society of Architectural Historians* 22: pp. 3–12.

1964 "La Bibliotheca Hertziana a Roma." *Duemila, Rivista Italo-Tedesca* 1: pp. 64–65.

1964 "Notizen zum kirchlichen Zentralbau der Renaissance." *Studien zur toskanischen Kunst, Festschrift für Ludwig Heinrich Heydenreich.* pp. 157–165. Munich.

1964 "La Sosta di Goethe a Caserta." *Archivio Storico di Terra di Lavoro* 3: pp. 633–636.

1964 With J. S. Ackerman. "Vignoliana." *Essays in Memory of Karl Lehmann (Marsyas,* Supplement I): pp. 1–24. Locust Valley, N.Y.

1965 "Der Bildhauer Aegidius von Wiener Neustadt in Padua." *Studien zur Geschichte der europäischen Plastik, Festschrift für Theodor Muller.* pp. 105–112. Munich.

1965 "Zu Michelangelos Christus in S. Maria sopra Minerva." *Festschrift für Herbert von Einem.* pp. 143–150. Berlin.

1966 "Riflessioni sul tema Palladio Urbanista." *Bollettino del Centro Internazionale di Studi di Architettura 'Andrea Palladio'* 8: pp. 123–127.

1966 "La Trasformazione Sansoviniana di Piazza S. Marco e l'urbanistica del Cinquecento." *Bollettino del Centro Internazionale di Studi di Architettura 'Andrea Palladio'* 8, no. 2: pp. 114–122.

1967 "Zur Erinnerung an Walter Friedlaender." *Mitteilungen des Kunsthistorischen Instituts in Florenz* 13: p. 194.

1967 "Der Palazzo Zuccari in Rom: Ein Künstlerhaus des 16. Jahrhunderts als Sitz eines Max-Planck-Instituts." *Jahrbuch 1967 der Max-Planck-Gesellschaft zur Förderung der Wissenschaften e. V.* pp. 149–155.

1967 "Palladio e Sansovino." *Bollettino del Centro Internazionale di Studi di Architettura 'Andrea Palladio'* 9: pp. 13–23.

1967 "Sansovinos Bibliothek von S. Marco und die Stadtbaukunst der Renaissance." *Kunst des Mittelalters in Sachsen, Festschrift für Wolf Schubert.* pp. 336–343. Weimar.

1968 "Italienische Plätze des 16. Jahr-
hunderts." *Jahrbuch 1968 der
Max-Planck-Gesellschaft zur
Förderung der Wissenschaften e.
V.* pp. 41–60.

1969 "Bernini e la Scalinata di Piazza
di Spagna." *Colloqui del Sodalizio*
ser. 2, no. 1: pp. 100–110.

1969 "Die Spanische Treppe: Archi-
tektur als Mittel der Diplomatie."
*Römisches Jahrbuch für Kunst-
geschichte* 12: pp. 39–94.

1972 "Die Piazza Ducale von Vigevano: Ein fürstliches Forum des
späten 15. Jahrhunderts." *Kunsthistorische Forschung: Otto Pächt
zu Ehren.* pp. 243–257. Salzburg.

1972 "Rudolf Wittkower (Berlin 1901–
New York 1971)." *Arte Veneta*
25: p. 304.

1973 "Inaugurazione della mostra di
Jacopo Barozzi 'Il Vignola' nel
quarto Centenario della morte"
(Vignola, 10 November). pp.
1–9.

1973 "Gli 883 cocchi della Roma del
1594." *Studi Offerti a Giovanni
Incisa della Rocchetta. Miscellanea
della Società Romana di Storia
Patria* 23: pp. 247–266.

1973 "L'Opera del Vignola." *Catalogo
della Mostra di Jacopo Barozzi
detto 'Il Vignola'.* pp. 40–55.
Vignola.

1973 "Palladio e l'architettura del suo
tempo." *Palladio, Catalogo della
Mostra.* pp. 27–30; 33–42.
Vicenza.

1973–"Bramante and the Quattro-
1974 cento Cloister." *Gesta* 12:pp.
111–121.

1974 With L. H. Heydenreich. *Architecture in Italy, 1400–1600.*
Pelican History of Art. Harmondsworth and Baltimore.

1974 "Introduzione ai lavori del Convegno." *Atti del Convegno Internazionale: Galeazzo Alessi e
l'Architettura del Cinquecento.* pp.
9–12. Genoa.

1974 "La Piazza Ducale di Vigevano:
Un foro principesco del tardo
Quattrocento." *Studi Braman-
teschi: Atti del Congresso Interna-
zionale* [1970], Milan, Urbino,
Rome, pp. 205–221.

1974 "I Desegni." *La Vita e le Opere
di Jacopo Barozzi da Vignola.*
pp. 125–167. Vignola.

LIST OF ILLUSTRATIONS

INTRODUCTION

These collected essays, mostly in translation from German and Italian originals, represent a selection of the shorter writings of Wolfgang Lotz which illustrate most effectively his contribution to the understanding of Italian Renaissance architecture. They illuminate a career at the forefront of modern scholarship and criticism: the first of them, for example, in the twenty years since its publication has exerted a pervasive influence on writing and teaching in the field and has come to be recognized as a classic of architectural history.

Wolfgang Lotz was born in Heilbronn, Germany, in 1912 and studied Art History, first at Munich and then at Hamburg, where he took his doctoral degree in 1937, writing a thesis entitled *Vignola Studies,* a subject to which he has returned often. His postdoctoral fellowship at the German Institute of Art History in Florence developed into a three-year research assistantship there, which was terminated in 1942 by a call to military service on the Eastern front. He was assigned ultimately as an interpreter of English, a language he claims to have been unable to speak at the time. Captured in 1945 by American troops, he was soon cleared and released to work for the International Commission for Monuments, Fine Arts, and Archives. During the following five years he helped found and administer the new Central Institute for the History of Art in Munich; then, though he qualified in 1953 for a post on the Munich University faculty, he accepted an offer to begin his teaching career as the successor to Richard Krautheimer at Vassar College. In 1959, he followed Krautheimer to the Institute of Fine Arts of New York University, the largest American graduate school in the field, and also taught in the undergraduate college. Three years later he accepted the Directorship of the Hertziana Library in Rome, a major center of scholarship and the finest European research library in the field of Italian art. He has made the Hertziana into an intellectual center for scholars and students of all countries. Most recently, he has returned to the United States to assume the Kress Professorship in residence at the National Gallery, Washington, D.C., for the fall and winter of 1976.

Lotz wrote recently that he was drawn to the United States "partly by a left-over dream from the Nazi years and partly by my great esteem for Richard Krautheimer," adding that the rigidity of the traditional European academic structure and his antipathy to the philosophical slant of the chief art historian at Munich University were also propelling forces. His informality and flexibility disposed him to find himself at home in this country, and his writing already had a pragmatism, a simplicity, and an openness to new approaches that were in tune with American scholarly attitudes. Because of his readiness to attack a particular problem on whatever terms he feels are best suited to it, it is not possible to label the school or style to which the following studies belong; each is somewhat different in method and import, and the totality does not illustrate a doctrine. There are, of course, underlying predilections that in some way identify the author with the most perceptive critic-historians of his generation, such as his attraction to the symbolic content of buildings and urban areas and his awareness of how the artist's modes of perception affect his approach to design problems. And there are constants of method, the most explicit in this group of studies being the dependence on drawings as a source for understanding the architect and his work. The following comments on each of the essays are intended to explain what I think makes them worth reading and studying, and something of their position in relation to other writing on Renaissance architecture.

The importance of the first essay, "The Rendering of the Interior in Architectural Drawings of the Renaissance," is obscured by the modesty of its announced aim—to trace the evolution of the representation of the interior of projected or executed buildings during the Renaissance. In following three generations of draftsmen as they struggled with the insoluble conflict between renderings that satisfied the desire for a convincing illusion and those that provided accurate measurements for builders, the study penetrates deeply into the psychology of Renaissance architects and discovers a key to the ways in which they intended their buildings to be seen. Illusionism in architectural rendering demanded perspective representation of buildings according to methods derived from the "costruzione legittima" invented by Brunelleschi and codified by Alberti in his book on painting of 1435. Lotz shows us how architecture followed the lead of painting—partly because almost all Renaissance architects were trained as painters or sculptors—and how, as a consequence, paintings (and especially those representing buildings) can be used as evidence for approaches to

architecture. But he also shows us that Alberti, writing his theory of architecture in about 1450, recommended that designers construct models as a
way of visualizing a building in three dimensions from many points of
view; additionally, they should make plans and elevations drawn, not according to his perspective method but by orthogonal projection, which,
because it flattens all planes to the single surface of the drafting paper, is
nonillusionistic. The orthogonal elevation permits every element to be
shown at the same scale, so that the carpenter and the mason can work from
it; it remains today the chief mode of rendering. Alberti did not explain
how to make such drawings, and it took nearly seventy years of experiment
to perfect the technique. In tracing the steps to the final solution by Antonio
da Sangallo the Younger—significantly the first Renaissance architect
trained in the profession—Lotz demonstrates how the drawings reveal the
changing attitudes toward space, mass, and movement from Leonardo
through Bramante, Peruzzi, and Raphael, and suggests that the huge scale
and complex design of the Basilica of St. Peter's in Rome demanded new
kinds of draftsmanship to make the structural problems controllable. This
essay is a model for the analysis of architectural drawing of any period, and
to the extent that it reveals an evolution of perception, its revelations are
referable to aspects of Renaissance culture other than architecture.

"Notes on the Centralized Church of the Renaissance" takes up a theme
that occupied the most distinguished historians of medieval and Renaissance
architecture before Lotz. Jakob Burckhardt distinguished the central-plan
church as a type in the first handbook of Renaissance architecture; André
Grabar and Richard Krautheimer traced the symbolism of martyria and
Marian churches from antiquity through the Middle Ages. More recently,
Rudolf Wittkower discussed the concepts of Renaissance theoreticians who
dealt with the type, while Lotz's lifelong associate, Ludwig Heydenreich,
for whose *Festschrift* this essay was written, examined the central-plan
churches of Leonardo da Vinci in his doctoral dissertation. But while the
issue is familiar in Lotz's sequence of five "Notes," a wholly new interrela-
tionship is established among the several components of the Renaissance
architect's attraction to round, domed churches: their formal role as freestanding monuments visible from afar, their medieval iconographical antecedents, and the peculiarly Renaissance conflict between the demands—
esthetic and structural—of the interior and the exterior appearance of the
dome, cogently stated by Leonardo da Vinci in an observation on the dome
problem. The fact that nearly every Renaissance dome from the Cathedral

of Florence to St. Peter's in the Vatican was built with an internal shell of low profile (for structural stability and a satisfactory internal appearance), and an external shell that springs from a higher base and rises in a more elevated profile (for visibility and impressiveness at a distance), has rarely been explained at all, and never as felicitously as here. The essay is a brief sequel to one of Lotz's major contributions to Renaissance scholarship, the book-length article of 1955 entitled "Oval Church Interiors of the Cinquecento," which demonstrates how in the later Renaissance the central-plan church was often extended along one axis to become oval, thereby attaining at once the symbolic virtues of the circle and the liturgical advantages of the longitudinal form, with its focus on the altar.

Two of the essays deal with Renaissance urban design, a subject that has begun only recently to attract architectural historians of the period: "Sixteenth-Century Italian Squares" and "The Piazza Ducale in Vigevano: A Princely Forum of the Late Fifteenth Century." Lotz's introduction to the first essay on squares suggests that contemporary concerns for the form of the city may have sparked his interest, and particularly the currently much-debated question of how to preserve the quality of old cities in the process of remaking them to suit new needs. The study shows how much Renaissance designers not only retained the historic form of public squares, and often the medieval buildings bordering them, but attempted to make their new structures conform in character, if not in vocabulary, to the remains of the past. Though the sixteenth-century vocabulary was classical, Lotz shows how ingeniously a conflict between respect for the medieval past and the principles of ancient planning (especially the framing of open areas by loggias) was coordinated with the character of existing cities. The solution differed in almost every town because history had left different traces in each case, and because the utopian schemes of theorists like Filarete—which would have provided uniformity—were rarely realized. Lotz's approach to urban design, with its emphasis on historical evolution as a formative force and on the political and economic determinants of design decisions, veers sharply from that of earlier writers, who generally approached the subject from an exclusively esthetic viewpoint.

One Renaissance square is studied in depth in the following piece "The Piazza Ducale in Vigevano." This square differs from most of the others in being a scheme that wiped away the traces of the past to create an ideal environment wholly shaped by a distinguished patron and a prominent architect, Ludovico Maria Sforza and Bramante. Because of this, it has been discussed as an abstract work of art—so much so that in earlier studies the piazza is usually illustrated without indications of the surrounding town of which it is the core. Lotz characteristically does not set out with the purpose of altering that critical tradition; he introduces the square by describing the site and then examining the arcades surrounding the open space on three sides (the fourth is occupied by the cathedral), noting that while substantial changes have occurred over the centuries there is evidence on the buildings and in some old watercolors for reconstructing the original state. There is also an inscription saying that Ludovico il Moro, Duke of Milan, suppressed "external and internal disorders," repaired the castle alongside, and built a large and beautiful square. Investigating the history of the "disorders" Lotz finds that the citizens, seeking to retain communal freedoms, were subdued by the Dukes of Milan. Step by step it emerges that the square, pointedly called the Piazza Ducale, and the castle are symbols of Sforza domination and that major features of the decorative scheme are intended to underscore this fact. This conclusion does not invalidate an appreciation of the formal qualities of its architecture, but it demonstrates the inadequacy of criticism that focuses exclusively on such appreciation. The essay modestly but vividly illustrates the new breadth of perspective in the best recent scholarship, which encompasses all available evidence of past cultures and consciousness and no longer stops short at the artificial borderline between art and history, literature, economics, politics, and biography; moreover, it properly draws architecture into a social realm, where new value considerations can come to the fore.

Italian scholars of a theoretical bent use the term "philological" to describe nit-picking documentary scholarship that is concerned only with minutiae, while missing the quality and meaning of works of art. This makes it more difficult to speak admiringly of a philological method that illuminates the inventive processes of a designer and enriches our understanding through the systematic study of his architectural vocabulary and syntax, and its origins. But it is the proper term for characterizing Lotz's exemplary study of "The Roman Legacy in Sansovino's Venetian Buildings." Previous writers on Sansovino's Library of San Marco and related designs have not succeeded in demonstrating satisfactorily how these related to earlier architectural thought, perhaps because none of them knew so well the Roman ambience of Sansovino's early career. The key to Lotz's unique command of this subject and others, from his earliest writing on, is his realization that architects' drawings are as important as executed buildings as evidence of their intentions and thought processes. No earlier scholar had acquired such a thorough experience of the thousands of surviving architectural drawings of the sixteenth century (there are several hundred by Antonio da Sangallo the Younger alone in the Uffizi, some of which are crucial to the Sansovino essay). In almost every study by Lotz, drawings from this vast corpus have played a significant role and, through his critical interpretations, have significantly extended our view of Italian Renaissance architecture.

The evidence of drawings and engravings was surely basic to the reformulation of the evolution of architectural style in the sixth essay, entitled "Italian Architecture in the Later Sixteenth Century." This impressive effort to redefine the main currents of later Renaissance architecture rejects both the earlier characterization of the period as proto-Baroque (suggested by Wölfflin's *Renaissance and Baroque*) and the more recent designation as Mannerist (notably in celebrated essays of Nikolaus Pevsner and Rudolf Wittkower). Its chief virtue, as in many other instances in this volume, is in casting off the respected formulas for addressing its subject, rejecting a mental set. The kernel of the argument is that mid-sixteenth century Italian architecture was classicist, purist, often static, balanced, and cool. Vignola emerges as the theorist and principal practitioner of the style. And the essay is as remarkable for what it does not say as for what it does; it entirely avoids the concept of Mannerism, which had dominated discussion of late Renaissance architecture. This is in part because Lotz wanted his characterization to encourage a fresh look at the buildings and drawings, and in part perhaps because he believes that the concept of Mannerism, invented to define tendencies in the figural arts, is ill-adapted to much of the architecture of the period. The interpretation of the Pitti Palace in Florence is striking in this respect. While other modern critics had defined it as Mannerist because of its tense and artificial rustication, Lotz sees beyond the surface to a static, classicistic structure. Even Michelangelo's design of the Capitoline Hill in Rome he interprets as being classicistically focused on its central equestrian monument (which seems to me forced, but some extreme positions are necessary in making a bold effort to redefine an entire period).

The "Three Essays on Palladio," which comprise the last chapter of the book, have been selected from a number of Lotz's contributions at the annual seminars held at the Centro Internazionale di Studi dell'Architettura "Andrea Palladio" in Vicenza, which is housed in one of Palladio's palaces.

Lotz is now the chairman of the committee of specialists guiding the activities of this center, which, since its foundation some twenty years ago, has been a vigorous force in promoting studies of Palladio and other architects of his time, and of problems of urbanization in the Veneto. Two of the three pieces should be read in the light of the veritable industry of Palladio scholarship promoted by the Center, because they are, in a sense, curatives. "Reflections on Palladio as Town Planner" answers a number of authors who have made inflated claims for Palladio's contributions to that field. It says, in effect, that the architect was not fundamentally concerned with creating cohesive urban settings but rather wanted his buildings, like the Basilica and the Loggia in Vicenza, to be seen as independent monuments. The second essay, "Observations on Palladio's Drawings," is a reflection on the drawing catalogue published in 1959 by Giangiorgio Zorzi, a scholar of the last generation who has devoted his life to the study of Palladio. The catalogue contains controversial reattributions of a large number of Palladio drawings to the contemporary Paduan architect Falconetto, on what is widely felt to be insufficient grounds. Lotz here manages unobtrusively to restore the credit to Palladio as a byproduct of his further penetration into an understanding of the corpus, demonstrating for the first time that many Palladian and other Renaissance drawings—particularly of antique buildings—were copies of drawings done by earlier architects, or even pastiches from several such sources. The final piece, "The Rotonda: A Secular Building with a Dome," should be read as a complement to the second essay, "Notes on the Centralized Church of the Renaissance." It seeks to explain why, if the dome is an ecclestiastical form with specific symbolic content as discussed in that essay, it should be employed in a suburban secular building. The answer is that in the course of the Renaissance the dome came to have an esthetic as contrasted to a symbolic meaning, that it bespoke "monument" so that its use was indicated to monumentalize domestic as well as ecclesiastical architecture, and particularly when it was sited, as at the Villa Rotonda, so as to be visible from all sides. The explanation was particularly valuable to critics of Renaissance and later architecture because of the unparalleled influence of the Villa Rotonda on subsequent architecture, which scattered its offspring throughout the world.

I am truly grateful that The M.I.T. Press has taken the initiative in bringing out this volume; first, because through its penetrating commentary on a wide variety of specific issues in Italian Renaissance architecture, it provides an insight that cannot be had in a general survey—even one as thorough as Lotz's *Italian Architecture 1400–1600*, published with L. H. Heydenreich in 1974—and second, because Wolfgang Lotz deserves this celebration of his achievement in the country where he spent almost his entire teaching career and to which he has contributed so much of worth.

James S. Ackerman
Harvard University

STUDIES IN
ITALIAN RENAISSANCE
ARCHITECTURE

1
THE RENDERING OF THE INTERIOR
IN ARCHITECTURAL DRAWINGS OF THE
RENAISSANCE

Our purpose is to discuss the two methods by which the interior is rendered in architectural drawings of the Early and High Renaissance: the perspective section and the section with orthogonal projection. Both methods represent the building as if bisected by an imaginary plane. As a rule the perspective view uses a single vanishing point and assumes a single viewer. The floor, walls, and vaults beyond the section plane appear foreshortened, as if seen from either above or below, just as a viewer from a vantage point on this side of the section plane would see them. On the other hand, the orthogonal view gives an unforeshortened representation of those parts of the building that lie beyond the section plane and are parallel to it. Curved or slanting walls or vaults are projected on the sectional plane with their foreshortening represented as if an imaginary viewer were seeing every part of the building straight on. The orthogonal section is generally shaded—to help distinguish the degree of recession of the planes represented—indicating in most cases that light enters from the left of the viewer. The use and development of both methods in the Italian Renaissance are closely allied with the conception and form of the interior (Fig. A).

Whereas in France and Germany numerous architectural drawings made in the fifteenth and sixteenth centuries have been preserved, there is nothing comparable from Florence, nor indeed from the whole of central Italy.[1] We have never come across a drawing by an architect which could be dated with certainty before about 1460; the earliest drawings that have come down to us date from the last quarter of the century, and the problem

This essay grew out of a lecture the author first gave in connection with the exhibition *Plan und Bauwerk,* Munich, 1952, and subsequently delivered in a somewhat altered form at Harvard University in the winter of 1953. After completion of the manuscript, I became acquainted with R. Wittkower's papers on "Brunelleschi and Proportion in Architecture," and, "The Perspective of Piero della Francesca's *Flagellation," Journal of the Warburg and Courtauld Institutes* 16(1953):pp. 275–302. This essay was published as "Das Raumbild in der Architekturzeichnung der italienischen Renaissance," in *Mitteilungen des Kunsthistorischen Instituts in Florenz* 7(1956), pp. 193–226

A. Perspective and orthogonal rendering of an interior
(1) One-point perspective of an interior
(drawing: Peter Haas)

(2) The same interior represented as
section with orthogonal projection
(drawing: Peter Haas)

of whether Brunelleschi and Alberti drew the plans and interiors of their buildings and, if so, how they went about it, can be clarified only by the written sources.

Brunelleschi's famous perspectives of the Piazza Signoria and the Baptistry in Florence can be used here only as collateral evidence. They treated exterior views alone and are not architectural drawings in the narrowest sense; that is, they did not serve in the planning, the execution, or the illustration of a building project, nor was it Brunelleschi's intention to represent these buildings for their own sake, as examples of outstanding architecture.[2]

The much-quoted passage in Alberti's *Ten Books on Architecture*,[3] which defines the difference between drawings made by painters and those done by architects, is of greater significance here: "Between the mode of depiction of painters and architects there is this difference, that the painter achieves an appearance of relief on his panel by shadows and the fore-shortening of lines and angles, while the architect, avoiding shadows, gets his relief from the drawing of the plan, and indicates in other drawings the form and measurement of the facade and sides by lines of invariable length and real angles, since he does not want his work judged by illusory appearance but precisely on the grounds of determinate quantities."[4] Perspective and shading, while indispensable to the painter for a truthful, theoretically correct representation of three-dimensional forms on a two-dimensional plane, are at best permissible to the architect only as an expedient. His truth lies in the *proportio* and *divisio*—proportion and principal measurements—of the second *and* third dimension which, according to Alberti, can be represented only in the ground plan; in a perspective rendering of necessity they must appear distorted and hence "untruthful."

One might consider these ideas of Alberti as a theoretical justification for a practice already long in existence. Were his statement applied to the well-known drawing of Milan Cathedral now in Bologna (Fig. 1),[5] Alberti's words could serve almost as a text for the method of representation used. No elements of perspective are present. In the ground plan the interior appears to be bounded by an abstract membrane stretched between the piers; the section shows only the skeleton of the building—piers and vaults—and this in such a way that the principal measurements, Alberti's *divisiones,* can be read clearly. In such drawings, exact measurements can be dispensed with: "With the sole exception of the ground measurements, all the measurements are of a purely geometric nature . . . which, even if they were to be calculated in the old foot units, would only yield irrational figures."[6] In the words of Alberti, however, they represent "true division based on *ratio*." As Heinrich von Mügeln, the court poet of Emperor Charles IV, expressed it: "The art of geometry teaches us measurement."[7] Alberti concedes the use of the perspective as an auxiliary to the architect. In his opinion, however, the proper medium for the representation of a building is the model: "I always recommend the ancient builders' practice by which not only drawings and pictures but also wooden models are made, so that the projected work can be considered and reconsidered, with the counsel of experts, in its whole and in all its parts."[8]

Here again Alberti describes practices that are confirmed in numerous written sources from the fourteenth and fifteenth centuries.[9] Brunelleschi, for instance, when he planned Santo Spirito, began by submitting "a design upon which the foundations [the ground plan] were based and with which he told them verbally how it would appear three-dimensionally."[10] This means that neither an elevation nor a *dipintura*—an interior drawn in perspective—was needed for these discussions. Only oral explanations on the part of the architect were necessary. After the building authorities had made their decision, Brunelleschi received "a commission to make, or have made, a small-size model in wood."[11] This shows most clearly that, in strict accordance with Alberti's later treatise, a ground plan and a model were considered indispensable for the planning and execution of a building. Even for such a large and complex building project as Santo Spirito in Florence elevations were considered unnecessary. The procedure was different for smaller and simpler buildings. With reference to the Ospedale degli Innocenti, Manetti reports that Brunelleschi "provided . . . a design on a small scale and with exact measurements; . . . for the portico of which the drawing alone sufficed without a wooden model."[12] Here, where it was not a matter of a complex interior of a large church, an elevation with appended scale dimensions was considered sufficient. Nevertheless Manetti's wording seems to imply that this was an unusual case; the fact that the master masons and carvers who were in charge and to whom Brunelleschi explained his drawing later deviated from his design is further confirmation of this. Manetti's description of the "principal weaknesses and discrepancies, very evident from the design that Filippo had left" is well known.[13]

In view of the foregoing it will come as no surprise that the earliest known drawing that shows an interior in perspective constructed precisely according to rule is the work of a painter: a drawing by Pisanello, show-ing the interior of a room covered by a barrel vault (Fig. 2).[14] The con-struction of the vanishing point and of the horizon corresponds exactly to the precepts of Alberti's treatise *On Painting:* "This point is properly placed when it is no higher from the base line of the quadrangle than the height of the man I have to paint there. Thus, both the beholder and the painted things he sees will appear on the same plane."[15] Pisanello's drawing clearly shows the advantages offered by this method for establish-ing the scale and placement of the figures within an architecturally defined space. The vertical and horizontal construction lines can be used as wall pilasters and for the pattern of the floor pavement; at the same time they fix the relative scale of the figures. Pisanello obviously did not intend to design or copy a specific interior in this drawing; rather, he used it as a setting for his human figures, as advocated by Alberti. The barrel vault is continued into infinity and there is no attempt to represent a closed room as it would appear in real life. Significantly, only the figures are shaded, while the architecture remains a totally abstract skeleton. The placing of the vanishing point in the middle axis, following Alberti's precepts, has the advantage of permitting the representation of simple interiors without overlapping.

Giuliano da Sangallo's drawing of the interior of the Hagia Sophia (Fig. 3), which he copied from the sketchbook of Ciriaco d'Ancona,[16] similarly shows that the "transparency" or nonexistence of the wall was at least nothing unusual to an architect of the late Quattrocento. He still drew the interior with foreshortenings and shadings in the manner of Villard d'Honnecourt.[17] Of course Ciriaco d'Ancona's perspective must have appeared out of date to a late Quattrocento artist, yet Giuliano da Sangallo, trained as he was in the tradition of Brunelleschi, did not hesitate to reproduce the older drawing unaltered in his collection of famous buildings. This Codex Barberini will be discussed more fully later in this essay.

Numerous architectural views in the sketchbooks of Jacopo Bellini are similar to the Pisanello drawing. Here, too, perspective is usually carried to infinity. The draftsman is not concerned with rendering an interior but uses the architectural forms as a convenient foreshortening scale for his figures. As a rule these drawings show simple, barrel-vaulted interiors,[18] in which the shape of the room and the arrangement of the figures corre-spond exactly to Pisanello's scheme.[19] In the rare instances where more complex buildings are drawn, they are shown always in frontal view, so that the perspective image can be grasped more readily.

The impact of Alberti's work *On Painting* on North Italian painting during the later Quattrocento is documented in Bellini's representations of architecture. Because they are the works of a painter who created them merely as a backdrop for his figures, they fall outside the scope of this essay. It has been recognized in the sketchbooks of Bellini that "the art-historical principles of L. B. Alberti are most logically realized. This becomes most clearly evident in their treatment of 'equidistant' and 'collinear' planes, in the subdivision of ceiling and floor into squares, each side of which measures one ell, and in the use of various high planes."[20] The fact that architectural perspectives were a favorite motif in North Italian painting makes it all the more remarkable that they were lacking in architectural plans.

Filarete's *Treatise on Architecture* also reveals Alberti's influence, both in its methodology of architectural planning and in its manner of representing a building in a drawing. After the architect first has prepared "a linear design showing the foundations" that the patron has accepted, he then must produce "a model, which one might also call a design in three dimensions."[21] The main purpose of the model is to present the project visually to the patron a second time. This requires further verbal explanation. In Filarete's description of the architect's practice there is no mention of elevations or drawings in perspective. The rendering of houses in perspective is not discussed until almost the end of his *Treatise,* and then only to demonstrate Filarete's own method. He first explains the foreshortening of human figures in a picture, then of square, round, and polygonal buildings, and finally of animals on a reduced scale.[22]

Nevertheless, the Florentine copy of Filarete's manuscript[23] contains what appears to be the earliest perspective interior view drawn by a Tuscan architect of the Renaissance. This is a representation of the fantastic House of Virtues (Fig. 4),[24] a many-storied structure over a circular ground plan consisting of a winding central staircase in the form of a tower surrounded by two concentric rings of loggias. Filarete explains that the two loggias could be shown only in sections: "The shaft [spiral staircase] cannot be drawn, unless it was made projecting; therefore, it is necessary for the mind to comprehend its particular form."[25] This remark makes it clear how much the drawing was an insufficient substitute for the actual model.

The curved line below the section denotes the ground plan of the House of Virtues. The vantage point of the viewer is moved away from the building and is placed at about the height of the second story; however, the perspective construction is not carried out accurately, as otherwise the upper stories would have to appear more strongly foreshortened than the lower ones. Thus Filarete's perspective is less correct in Quattrocento terms—that is, less "truthful"—than those of Pisanello and Jacopo Bellini.

Another drawing in Filarete's *Treatise* shows the loggias with which Filarete intended to surround the marketplace of Sforzinda (Fig. 5).[26] In this drawing the arcade's rear wall and the vaults are shaded, probably to give a maximum three-dimensional effect to the columns. In other respects, too, the illustration betrays the tendency to stress the subdivisions of the loggia rather than the walls. In the House of Virtues, for instance, the exterior walls are so thin they bring to mind modern steel construction, and there is no indication as to how the interior would look. Like the artist who, around 1400, drew the ground plan and elevation of Milan Cathedral, Filarete thought of the space-limiting wall as "abstract"—as a nearly superfluous plane surface—and not as a massive enclosing element. The artistic interest is still focused on the *divisiones* of the walls, which cannot be shown adequately in a perspective drawing.

The illustration of the market loggia shows very clearly that the illustrator of the *Treatise* was well acquainted with the use of perspective. Next to the loggia the drawing provides a glimpse of an interior, which possibly forms part of the *Beccaria* described in the *Treatise*. The actual loggia is shown from a bird's-eye view with a comparatively high horizon, while the side room is represented with a different vanishing point and a lower horizon, additional proof that the illustrator did not use perspective for its own sake, but as a means of demonstrating his point, and that he used it unsystematically. This is exactly what the text of the *Treatise* suggests. Where the drawings are mentioned at all, they are intended to serve the artist for the instruction of his princely patron in the field of architecture. However, they are not considered scientifically correct renderings of the buildings, indispensable to the architect, nor are they seen as working drawings.

An examination of drawings representing Romanesque buildings in Florence, ascribed for good reasons to Simone Cronaca, leads us to similar conclusions.[27] When rendering the wall of the nave of the church of SS. Apostoli (Fig. 6), the draftsman delineates only the contours of the columns and the outlines of the clerestory windows, completely omitting any indication of frames around the windows, arcades, or aisle wall. The three-dimensional appearance of the wall and the volume of the space could have been articulated visually only through the use of perspective and shading. To speak in the words of Alberti, however, both would have resulted in an "apparente prospettiva"—an illustration in the manner of a painter—that would have distorted the *ratio* and *divisio* of the wall.

The Filarete illustrations are seemingly the work of a dilettante, but in their own peculiar way they go beyond the perspectives of Pisanello and of Jacopo Bellini and also, as we have seen, of Alberti. They do this by placing the vantage point, not on the floor of the building represented, but on an imaginary higher plane. Although the origin of this type of perspective construction lies outside the scope of the essay, it can be observed that, as a result of its use, these drawings already contain elements of the so-called cavalier perspective, a method that was further developed during the last quarter of the Quattrocento. This method was favored especially in the rendering of centralized buildings, so characteristic of the period, and of antique monuments, which resemble them in type. Obviously, an interior could be represented by this method only if the building were shown bisected.

The earliest systematically constructed examples of this method, which henceforth we shall call *bird's-eye view*, are found in the oeuvre of Leonardo da Vinci, who began as a painter and who was largely responsible for developing the basic forms of plane and perspective architectural drawings.[28] It is significant, though, that for the most part Leonardo's studies for centralized buildings are limited to ground plans and exteriors drawn in perspective. Interiors are rarely shown, and only appear relatively late in his drawings. A typical example, from the Codex Atlanticus dated around 1490,[29] shows separate views of the exterior and interior of a centralized building (Fig. 7). The omitted half of the building, which would lie on the viewer's side of the sectional plane, is indicated by means of a ground plan, also drawn in perspective. Here the designer is primarily concerned with the skeleton of the building and the subdivisions of the wall. The fact that the ground floor ambulatory is not shown as it appears from the inside but only in the sectional plane and in the ground plan—in those parts of the drawing that represent the abstract rather than the visual appearance of the building—shows how little Leonardo was interested in illustrating the space-limiting function of the wall. No matter how strongly the exterior view stresses the three-dimensional physical appearance of a building, the old concept of an interior as a skeleton whose members signify the *divisiones* of the walls in between apparently persists unchanged.

For the same reason, Leonardo's section in bird's-eye view renounces shading almost entirely. It is not the appearance of the interior that matters but the clarification of the relation between elevation and ground plan, and of the geometric-stereometric configuration of the building, as shown so lucidly in the drawing. Whenever Leonardo uses shading in his perspectives,[30] it serves to differentiate between such details as an open loggia and the unbroken wall above it, which remains unshaded. However, he does not use shading to characterize projecting parts and recesses within the wall, in other words, the shape of the interior.

Francesco di Giorgio treats the section in bird's-eye view in almost the same manner as Leonardo does, with whose drawings he was probably quite familiar. The Turin manuscript of his treatise on architecture includes a drawing (Fig. 8)[31] that shows only the outer wall of the ambulatory of Santa Costanza as it appears in the ground plan and in the profile of the cornices. Its space-limiting function is not made visible, and there is no shading whatsoever. Another sketch of his, showing Santo Stefano Rotondo (Uffizi A 330; Fig. 9), illustrates how the method was employed when the building was drawn *in situ;* this is also a centralized building with an ambulatory in which only the arcades are stressed but not the space-enclosing wall. The artist chose to let the viewer's vantage point be higher than the pavement of the ground floor but lower than the main cornice, with the result that it lies approximately at eye level. Thus his perspective construction still follows the precepts of Alberti.

At the present stage of research we are not able to attribute the invention of a correct perspective section to any single artist in particular, nor do we know precisely when this happened. The data of the Leonardo drawings in which this method was used are as uncertain as is that of the related sketches by Francesco di Giorgio Martini; the question is complicated further by the fact that the method was used in drawings by the Bramante circle, and possibly by Bramante himself—an aspect we shall discuss later. Therefore we must be content to state that the earliest example of a systematic use of the method is found in drawings by artists working at the court of Lodovico il Moro in Milan.

Neither Leonardo's model designs nor Francesco di Giorgio's architectural sketches are working drawings in the strictest sense. Up to the end of the Quattrocento larger and more complex interiors were evidently plan-

ned and visualized by means of the model alone.[32] Not until around 1500
are there increasing indications of its replacement by a drawing of the
interior. To cite one example: the collection of architectural drawings published by Thomas Ashby under the title of "Codex Coner" and attributed
by him to Bramante's Roman school[33] includes, besides the Pantheon, views
of contemporary buildings such as Bramante's Tempietto, shown in bird's-
eye view (Fig. 10).

It is the nature of this procedure that the high horizon—the unnaturally
high imaginary vantage point—allows the viewer no opportunity to gain
an idea of actual size of the building represented. The viewer trying to find
a relationship between his own natural eye level and the height shown in
the drawing finds himself frustrated, as the building appears too distant for
such an attempt. This is basically true of all views in bird's-eye view. It is,
however, less evident if the foreground, the lower part of the sheet, is indicated as being the level on which both building and viewer stand; this
was the approach Leonardo took. The draftsman of the Codex Coner, on
the other hand, uses the illusionary qualities of the method to their limits
by confining his representation to those parts of the building that lie beyond
the plane of the section, which he makes visible by an abstract base line.
This line represents the border between the half of the building actually
shown and the neutral surface of the sheet. The viewer is specifically barred
from mentally filling in the parts of the drawing below the base line as
representing ground or pavement and thus relating them to his own vantage point. One looks into the building's interior as though through a glass
wall. Alberti characterizes the sectional plane across the visual pyramid
as a glass wall on which the painter's perspective appears—"on this surface
are presented the forms of things seen as if it were of transparent glass."[34]

This also explains why the interior views so characteristic of the Codex
Coner frequently give the impression of being pictorial and immutable.
By identifying the paper surface with the plane of the section and thus with
the border between the visible building parts and those that are "missing,"
the artist accepts completely the principles of Quattrocento painting as
postulated by Alberti. Leonardo's sketches, on the other hand, allow the
space represented imperceptibly to spill over into the area before the plane
of the section—the space in f ont of the observer. The observer finds himself placed at a high vantage point, from which he looks out toward and
into the building. Accordingly the section is conceptually completed by the
addition of a half ground plan on this side of the section plane (Figs.

4, 7). While in his highly characteristic way Leonardo struggles to achieve clarity in his representation and to make the illusion more readily intelligible to the viewer, the artist of the Codex Coner makes no attempt to conceal the illusionary character of the section.

Ashby based his attribution of the Codex to an artist of the Bramante circle mainly on the type of buildings selected for inclusion. But the manner of representing interiors also points toward Bramante. It presupposes the same spatial concept as that expressed in the choir of Santa Maria presso San Satiro in Milan, a concept of an interior to be seen in perspective and thus capable of being represented in perspective (Fig. 14). The Codex Coner also applies to architecture the same principles of representation by means of perspective that, according to Alberti, are characteristic for painters. And, finally, both the simulated choir and the sections in bird's-eye view stress the three-dimensional qualities of the space-limiting wall in an entirely new way. The artist of the Codex Coner sheets applies shading to every window frame and coffer, wall projection and wall recess, as well as to the inside of the cupolas. Evidently he is less concerned with the simple geometry of the walls, with their *ratio* and *divisio,* than with their volume and relief. The exterior view (Fig. 11) also places more emphasis on the physical appearance of the wall and on the three-dimensional qualities of its component parts than on the contours that determine the *divisiones* of their surfaces. A comparison of the rendering of a support and of the wall behind it in Francesco di Giorgio's drawing (Fig. 9) with the columns and niches of the Pantheon in the Codex Coner (Figs. 12, 13) brings out the difference very clearly. The wall behind the columns is now strongly shaded; it is no longer an abstract plane, stretched, as it were, between supporting members.

In Santa Maria presso San Satiro and above all in the choir (Fig. 14), the continuance of the entablature around the supporting members and the use of decorative motifs serve to emphasize in exactly the same way the wall relief more sharply than in comparable buildings of the preceding era. Characteristically, the coffers of the barrel vault in the nave and transept are painted, but in the choir they are stuccoed. While this admittedly heightens the illusion, its more significant purpose seems to be to give greater depth to the wall. No longer are we confronted with the unbroken planes of the early and middle Quattrocento with their simple *divisiones,* as shown so clearly in Pisanello's drawing; no longer is the criterion of a room the *ratio*—the simple, measurable planes, and the space which they encompass. Bramante's interior is defined by the projections and recesses of the wall, by the lights and shadows they create, and by the three-dimensional profile and the relief of the wall. This is why we meet the same concept of space, based on form and volume, in the perspective relief of the simulated choir of Santa Maria and in the drawings of the Codex Coner. In both cases space is indicated by its relation to the relief of the surrounding wall.

Alberti's objections to the rendering in perspective of an interior within the framework of an architectural drawing were justified as long as "walls and ceiling . . . served not only as a means to contain rooms but became effective as part of the scene and were so executed that the space limits were given expressive value as decorative surfaces."[35] The *divisiones* of such planes and the *ratio* of the room sections bounded by them cannot be represented adequately in a perspective view. However, once wall and space are considered as possessing bodily volume, Alberti's reservations prove invalid; under these conditions space can be rendered in perspective just as can a body itself; indeed it can only be so rendered. The new spatial concept that produced the simulated choir now also enabled the architect, in drawing his design, to represent such a room in perspective. This does not rule out his reliance on Alberti's precepts when he constructs his perspectives. In the sections of the Codex Coner as well as in the simulated choir in Milan the viewer is assigned a vantage point at some distance from the room shown. In the drawings the room appears as an immovable picture behind the plane of the section, which corresponds to Alberti's "transparent surface" cutting through the optical pyramid; the choir appears equally picturelike in the wall of the transept. And the niches of the transept wall adjacent to both sides of the choir repeat the motif in a minor key.

But none of these representations of interiors give the viewer a clue as to the true scale of the architecture represented. It is not by chance that they are devoid of people, whereas, for example, the Pisanello drawing (Fig. 2) combines the human figure with architecture and thus supplies a point of reference.

Architectural drawings made by painters are found so frequently during the Quattrocento that they can almost be considered the rule.[36] Therefore it is not surprising that Bramante, who had gone to Milan as a painter, was commissioned to design Santa Maria presso San Satiro. What is unusual, however, is the fact that the planning and execution of Bramante's choir were done by using working methods of a painter. It is hard to believe that the simulated choir was built without a working drawing in the full size of the original, which in turn was an enlargement of the perspective design. Tracing from a cartoon became the rule in fresco painting from about 1450 on.[37] Bramante applied the same method to architecture wherever it made sense.

The real significance of this procedure is illuminated by a statement made by Alberti. In his treatise *On Painting* he ranks the painter before the architect, "because the architect, if I am not mistaken, has taken from the painter the finials, the capitals, the base, the columns, the cornices and all the other admirable features of the building"; by this he means that the architect merely gives substance to the inventions of the painter. Consequently architecture is an art of lower rank, painting one of higher, "the master and flower of all the arts." This also explains why Alberti described architectural images in his work *On Painting* rather than in his *Ten Books on Architecture*.[38] Therefore, the simulated choir is the work of a painter in terms of the working method, and here Bramante resolves the most difficult task that Alberti could give to a painter: "And in truth they would learn, while circumscribing a surface with lines and while covering with colors the places which have been designed and completed, that nothing further need be sought and that here in this single surface several forms of surface are represented."[39] This applies equally to the simulated choir and to the perspective drawings of the Codex Coner.

This pictorial quality, the relationship of an image to a distant vantage point, remains characteristic of Bramante's Roman interiors;[40] even the Tempietto is calculated to have a perspective effect in spite of its being equally developed on all sides. A viewer, standing in front of the building, can see through the open portal both the altar, with the relief of the crucifixion of St. Peter in the predella, and the statue of the seated apostle. The original version of the plan called for the building to be surrounded by a circular loggia, and the visitor entering the courtyard would have glimpsed the building itself between two columns and the architrave (or arch?) of the enclosing loggia. Furthermore, in the center of this framed over-all view he would have seen the altar with the apostle's statue and the representation of his martyrdom. In this way the building itself and its iconographic significance as a monument erected over the very spot where the apostle suffered his martyrdom would have been revealed at a glance. The beholder would have had a true view of this image in its totality only by standing away from the building at a certain distance, on the central axis of the courtyard near the portal leading into it. From just this one point would he have comprehended simultaneously the monument in its entirety and its iconographic "legend."

These peculiar artistic methods appear in a different but no less forceful way in Bramante's choir of Santa Maria del Popolo (Fig. 15). One views the apse within a triple frame formed by the three graduated recesses of the arch, and this image is once more framed by the projecting pilasters and the arch of the bay lying before the apse. Strictly speaking the apse is not to be entered but is to be viewed from a vantage point that has been moved back and now is situated near the altar in the center of the choir chapel. From this spot the viewer can take in at one glance the apse, the epitaphs of the cardinals on the walls, and the fresco of the Assumption in the vault.

The perspective section as used in the Codex Coner, with its high horizon, its fixed vantage point for the viewer, and its artificial picture plane, is ideally suited to interiors that are primarily conceived as a picture the elements of which are optically related to a vantage point set at a certain distance. In Bramante's interiors the viewer is not so much invited to walk around as to take in a static perspective picture—a picture as immovable and remote as is the view of the Pantheon in the Codex, for example. Bramante's interiors not only resemble those of the Codex in the method of their representation, but also share the same lack of scale. The visitor to Santa Maria presso San Satiro is taken aback by the discrepancy between the apparent height and width of the choir as seen from the correct vantage point and its actual height as seen at close range, in other words, incorrectly. Likewise, if one looks at the section of the Tempietto, one finds it hard to reconcile the scale recorded by the draftsman with the impression left by its apparently monumental interior (Fig. 10). Furthermore, the visitor who enters the Tempietto is likely to experience a sense of disappointment at the contrast between the monumental effect of the exterior and the modest dimensions of the interior. Lack of scale is a correlate of the perspective construction; as we know, the section through the optical pyramid provides no clue to the true dimensions so long as there are no human figures in the picture.

The Codex Coner also contains a view of the Basilica of Maxentius in the Forum (Fig. 16). Even in this instance where a direct rendering would have been possible, obviating the necessity of a section, since only about half of the building was still standing, the artist represents the two lateral walls of the main room as bisected. Once more his aim is to represent the appearance of an interior, not to draw a prospect in the manner of Heemskerck. Therefore, he reconstructs those parts of the lateral walls that are in ruins, but he fails to restore the main vault. One is inclined to believe that the artist realized his own lack of logic. Contrary to his usual habit, he does not draw a base line but, like Leonardo, interprets the lower portion of his sheet as the floor, on which he sketches in the ground plan of one of the large supports. Could this lack of consistency be explained by the fact that the reconstructed vault would hardly have been represented in a perspective section?

In another respect, too, the drawing reveals the shortcomings of the perspective method, which Alberti had already recognized—the foreshortenings and overlappings. The walls separating the barrel-vaulted side aisles hide a window axis of the outer wall on either side, and the two lateral walls of the nave cannot be understood unequivocally, despite the reconstruction. While the section in bird's-eye view is adequate for the rendering of plain centralized interiors, as in the Pantheon, which the eye can easily take in at a glance, or Bramante's "picture" interiors, which assign a vantage point to the viewer, it is ill-suited to more complex centralized buildings or to longitudinal interiors, as in the Basilica of Maxentius. The fact that the draftsman of the Codex Coner modifies his method of representation when dealing with the Basilica of Maxentius tends to indicate that he was aware of the problem.

The close connection between the method of representation used in the Codex Coner and the esthetic principles underlying the Bramante interiors probably can be explained most easily by the fact that Bramante, while not the actual inventor of the section in bird's-eye view, nevertheless perfected and made systematic use of it. Furthermore, as Ashby and Angelis d'Ossat have tentatively suggested, the sections of the Codex may well be based on architectural drawings by Bramante himself. And there is additional evidence to support this assumption. The method is used, for instance, throughout the so-called sketchbook of Bramantino (Figs. 17, 18),[41] a collection of architectural drawings of antique, mostly Roman, buildings, which can be dated with a high degree of certainty to the years between 1503 and 1514. Since the draftsman was a Lombard, one may assume that he was acquainted with Bramante and his working methods. If this is so, it is not surprising that he habitually supplements the perspective section by a ground plan of the same building. The plane of the section is indicated either as a base line, as in the Codex Coner (Fig. 18), or is identified with the front wall of the building in such a way that the picture is framed by the lateral edge of the facade, which, incidentally, is omitted (Fig. 17). The interior itself is always represented with a high and relatively far removed horizon; the viewer is assigned the same unnaturally high vantage point as in the views of the Codex Coner.

A very similar perspective interior view is shown in the unique drawing of the Fugger Chapel in Augsburg, signed with the initials S L, which stand for Sebastian Loscher (Fig. 19).[42] The Italianate elements of this drawing, and thus of the chapel itself, have long been associated with Hans Burgkmair. On the basis of the method of representation, which corresponds exactly to that of the Bramante circle and specifically to the so-called Bramantino, the connection with northern Italy, implicit in this association, may well be narrowed down to Milan. Even Feuchtmayr's dating of the drawing between 1509 and 1512, coinciding with the last years of Bramante's life, would fit.[43]

The examples of interior views so far discussed, taken in conjunction with the written sources, permit the following conclusions:

1. The perspective view described by Alberti and used by the Bramante circle was originally employed only in exceptional cases for the rendering of an interior of existing or planned buildings. Above all it was considered the province of painters, and thus it occurs frequently in their drawings.

2. The Gothic method of the pure orthogonal projection generally in use north of the Alps was apparently employed only in northern Italy at the builders' workshop of the Milan Cathedral, which followed the Gothic tradition in any case; there are no examples from central Italy. To some extent the Cronaca drawings, which depict older buildings and are not drawn to scale, represent a transitional stage.

3. The new spatial concept, as revealed in Bramante's simulated choir and his Roman buildings, is contemporary with the adoption of the perspective view for the representation of interiors. In contrast to the interiors of the early Quattrocento, those of Bramante that emphasize volume can be rendered adequately in perspective.

4. No other method of representing interiors, and certainly not that of the section with orthogonal projection, can be found in the extant drawings of the Bramante circle.

5. The perspective drawings made by the Bramante circle project the interior upon the "transparent surface," a term coined by Alberti to

describe the plane formed by the section through the optical pyramid. Even Bramante's executed buildings, such as the interior of the Tempietto, offer a perspective view related to a vantage point at a distance.

In view of these observations, it is surprising to find that in the builders' workshop of St. Peter's the perspective section was not used only in another way but finally was replaced by a method that renders the interior in a basically different manner. We refer to a large group of drawings considered by Geymüller to have come from the Bramante studio or to have been commissioned by him, but which Frey dated to the period after Bramante's death, for reasons that seem convincing.[44] In Frey's opinion, the drawings refer to a design for the nave planned under the direction of Raphael.

Peruzzi's drawing (Uffizi A 161; Fig. 20) is an attempt to adapt the system of the Constantine Basilica to the nave of St. Peter's. It shows the floor as seen from above, with a relatively high horizon, much like the view of the antique building in the Codex Coner (Fig. 16). In contrast, the architrave of the small order appears as seen from below; the blocks of the entablature over the high columns are hardly foreshortened; this means that they are approximately rendered in orthogonal projection.

While this mingling of different perspectives might appear to be the result of a rapidly drawn sketch, Giuliano da Sangallo's drawing (Fig. 21),[45] which is similar in form, shows that Peruzzi's "incorrect" perspective methods also appear in the design of a fellow artist working on the St. Peter's project. Sangallo applies perspective to the rendering of the barrel-vaulted chapel, the embrasures of the clerestory windows, and the main vault; yet everything else is almost invariably shown in orthogonal projection. The floor of the nave is not made visible. The wall molding of each bay has its own vanishing point, which lies at about the height of the respective profile.

This multiple perspective results in a spatial effect basically different from that of the Codex Coner, which uses a central perspective with a fixed vantage point. The "transparent plane" between the image of the interior and the viewer is abandoned, so to speak. The image is no longer immovable; on the contrary, the viewer has the illusion of standing in the room and being invited to move around freely within it.

Giuliano da Sangallo's Codex Barberini,[46] the result of the master's active collecting over several decades, is of importance to our theme inasmuch as the method by which Sangallo renders a given interior varies greatly within the Codex. If these variations are regarded, not as accidental, but as representing evolutionary stages, we may at once conclude that the view of the Hagia Sophia (Fig. 3) copied from Ciriaco d'Ancona—after a model of the first quarter of the Quattrocento—was the first item in this collection. Interiors that Giuliano himself rendered are represented quite differently. To give a few examples: only one side of the octagon of the Florentine Baptistry is represented (fol. 34 *recto*); only one-half of the octagon wall of the Baptistry at the Lateran (fol. 31 *recto*); when he draws the Oratorium S. Crucis he shows "one face of one of the chapels," to use his own words—only the wall of one of the four hexagonal chapels adjacent to the corners of the cross.[47] In each instance the view of the interior is limited to a section of the wall and the viewer can only visualize the appearance of the interior by mentally adding the missing identical sections. The view of the Minerva Medica, where Sangallo adds the elevations of two *conchae* lying across from each other to the ground plan (fol. 6 *recto;* Fig. 22), is typical of this apparently early method of representation.

The antique centralized buildings that were in high favor around 1500 are represented quite differently; for example, the views and ground plans of the circular temple near Santa Maria in Cosmedin and the so-called Portumnus temple are shown side by side (fol. 37 *recto;* Fig. 23). In both instances the artist emphasizes the ruinous state of the buildings in a peculiar way. He represents the temple at Santa Maria in Cosmedin by a combination of elevation, perspective view of the interior (visible through an opening in the partly collapsed circular wall), and abstract section. Since other, somewhat later, views show this wall intact, Sangallo's representation can only be intepreted as a flight of fancy;[48] he simply renders the wall facing the viewer as if it were broken, in order to provide a partial view of the interior. The spatial appearance is quite clearly more important to him than the *divisio,* or wall structure, in which the artists of the drawings discussed earlier were predominantly interested.

It is unlikely that the same artist would in the same period use such different methods as the "one-wall elevation" and the imaginary glimpse inside a ruin. There is every reason to believe that the difference in method also implies a different date of origin.[49] The section of a centralized building (fol. 59 *verso;* Fig. 24), which has been assigned on the basis of technique to the latest drawings of the Codex Barberini,[50] probably may be placed at the end of this evolution. This drawing shows the same transition from a central perspective to an orthogonal projection that we have noticed already in Sangallo's drawing (Fig. 21). The floor is seen from above, but the bases of the columns, raised only a few steps above floor level, are seen from below. This is an example of "frog perspective," a method that invariably results in a sharp reduction of distance. The upper story of the building, however, does not show the abrupt foreshortening one would expect. Consequently, this drawing also shows elements of orthogonal projection; its interior seems to envelop the viewer in a manner reminiscent of the studies made by Giuliano and Peruzzi in connection with their designs for St. Peter's, to which we referred earlier.

In terms of mathematical precision, the method of construction employed by Giuliano in the two drawings is inferior to the sections of the Codex Coner, since it is not scientifically correct in Alberti's sense. Whereas Bramante's perspective choir in Milan and the method of projection used by the Bramante circle betray an intense preoccupation with the theoretical problems of perspective, Sangallo evidently developed his rendering of interiors empirically. At a certain stage this development led to a method which, though less correct in matters of construction, comes relatively close to that of the Bramante circle and testifies to a quite similar concept of interior space: we refer to the renderings of antique centralized buildings (fol. 37 *recto*) and to related drawings in the Codex Barberini. We are tempted to date this group around the year 1500 or shortly thereafter, the more so since it was precisely during these years that "archaeological" interest was focused on this type of building.

On the other hand, the reduction of distances, the mixing of different perspectives with elements of the orthogonal projection, the new spatial concept as evidenced by the designs of the Codex Barberini 59 *verso* and Uffizi A 131 must be interpreted as the final phase in this development. They show such a basically new concept of space and perspective that the question arises whether this change was not brought about by some outside influence, by the drawings of a master with a different background.[51]

Raphael succeeded Bramante as chief architect in charge of St. Peter's. The earliest description of the theory of the sections in orthogonal projection is found in Raphael's famous letter to Pope Leo X, written in 1519, concerning the representation of ancient Rome in drawings.[52] In it Raphael "established the method of architectural drawings and insisted upon a separate ground plan, elevation, and section":[53]

"And because the method of drawing that belongs more to the architect differs from that of the painter, I shall state what seems to me appropriate to understand all the measurements and to know how to find all the parts of a building without error. The drawing of buildings, so far as the architect is concerned, therefore should be divided into three parts, of which the first is the plan, or rather the ground plan, the second deals with the exterior . . . the third, with the interior."[54] [For the elevation] "always measuring the whole on a small scale, one should draw a line of the width of the base of the whole building, and from the center of this line another straight line which forms two right angles with either side; in this shall be the line of the center of the building."[55] [All vertical elements of the facade shall be included according to scale in a system of parallel verticals formed on the base line by the center line, the outline of the building, and other verticals; an analogous system of parallels to the base line is used for the horizontal elements.] "The third part of this drawing, which we have defined as the interior wall, . . . is no less necessary than the other two, and is made in the same way from the plan with parallel lines, like the wall of the exterior; and it shows one half of the building from the interior, as though it were divided in the middle."[56]

Looking back for a moment at the perspective sections in the Codex Coner, one sees that Raphael's method of representing a building amounts to an abandonment of the central perspective and its underlying spatial concept of a section through the optical pyramid, as defined by Alberti and carried out by Bramante in his simulated choir. Admittedly, Alberti had declared that an architect could not abstract his "compartments based on reason" from the perspective image. However, his advice to make a plan and a model can only be interpreted to mean that, in his opinion, elevation and section, though well known to the older practitioners (at least in the North), did not figure among the true forms of representation available to an architect. Since they contradicted his definition of the optical image, inevitably they appeared to him as untrue.

The Bramante circle, which conceived of enclosed space as something imbued with volume—as an independent entity, as it were—and not like Alberti as "compartments based on reason," could only represent this spatial volume according to Alberti's rules of perspective. The orthogonal section, as postulated by Raphael, would have led to an untrue reproduction, because Bramante's interiors must be seen as an image in perspective.

Raphael's systematic separation of exterior and interior view, his striving for a nonperspectival reproduction resulting in the renunciation of a single vantage point for the viewer, de rigueur since Alberti, can only be taken to mean that the viewer too now experiences space within a building in a different way; one might even say that a different attitude is expected of him. The Chigi Chapel in Santa Maria del Popolo, the only religious interior by Raphael that is still intact, cannot be taken in at a glance, as can Bramante's choir in the same church, built barely a decade earlier. While all parts of the choir are visible at a distance from the altar, a visitor to the Chigi Chapel must go inside, look about him, and lift his gaze up to the cupola. He needs the cumulative effect of many impressions in order to take in and truly comprehend the chapel interior. Such a visitor no longer feels himself "surrounded by inner walls from which emanates the picture-like effect of framed and thoroughly composed surfaces"; rather the interior of the chapel is a completely "inward-gravitating, abstract space, the emphasis of which lies in its center,"[57] giving him the feeling of being enclosed on all sides. The picture qualities of the space-limiting surfaces recede completely before this impact of space.

It is perhaps not by chance that the opening sentence of the paragraph in Raphael's letter which concerns us here—"the method of drawing that belongs to the architect differs from that of the painter"—carries a faint echo of Alberti's formulations, although the letter itself goes far beyond them. The tasks confronting Raphael upon his taking office as chief architect of the *fabbrica* of St. Peter's could not be carried out by following Alberti's precepts. The spatial complexities of main and secondary cupolas, the arrangement of large and small orders, the process of harmonizing the old and the new building that he took over from Bramante, could not be represented, let alone planned, by the mere use of a ground plan and a model.

Raphael's tenure at St. Peter's lasted only six years. It is, however, no coincidence that the designs for the basilica, dating from precisely these years, have always been considered masterpieces of graphic art.[58] For Raphael, who was first and foremost a painter, drawing was of course the natural medium for both the planning and the execution of a design. The incredible quantity of work produced during the last years of his life, and his posthumous influence, can be explained by his characteristic talent for organization. One can scarcely believe that Raphael did not also try, in a similar way, to put his ideas for the new St. Peter's on record by means of drawings.[59] For the purpose of understanding all the measurements and knowing how to find all the parts without errors, the older methods, by which Brunelleschi's and even Bramante's much simpler buildings still could be represented, of necessity appeared inadequate from the outset. Only the orthogonal projection could do justice to the rendering of such a building for the purpose of graphically representing the building as it stood and as it was planned. Therefore one might assume that Raphael's description of the orthogonal projection in his letter to Leo X was the result of theoretical studies concerning the problems of architectural drawings, especially as they involved the representation of an interior which grew out of his activities at St. Peter's. Burdened as he was with numerous other commissions, Raphael had to derive a method that could specify his architectural intentions so as to ensure the continuance of the work even during his absence. To achieve this goal he needed a second architect, one who could interpret the plans and supervise their execution on the site.

There is no conclusive evidence to support this hypothesis. However, it would throw light on the connection between a number of well-known phenomena, which until now could only be described individually and hence could never be fully explained:

1. In the course of the second decade of the sixteenth century the architectural sketching, especially the interior view with the spatial appearance, became drawn into the planning and building process in quite a new way, and was used to establish the building program.

2. None of the extant early designs for St. Peter's showing elevations can be dated with certainty within Bramante's term in office. The generation immediately following Bramante was but inadequately acquainted with his plans. As Geymüller has shown, the famous vellum plan (Uffizi A 1) was not identical with the final design; even at the time of Bramante's death no fully worked-out plan seems to have been available. Significantly Serlio does not include any plan of Bramante's and makes a point of explaining: "but the model on which many minds labored, including Raphael of Urbino, still remains imperfect in some parts."[60]

3. The multiple perspective used by Peruzzi and Giuliano da Sangallo in their studies connected with St. Peter's is the preliminary step of the orthogonal projection explained in Raphael's letter of 1519. The first artist to apply this projection correctly and consistently is Antonio da Sangallo the Younger, as will be shown later. These three masters were active at St. Peter's as Raphael's colleagues or assistants.

4. The organization of the *fabbrica* underwent considerable change during Raphael's tenure. While Bramante kept the planning and supervision of the building in his own hands, after his death the leading architect, Raphael, was granted assistants: first Giuliano da Sangallo and Fra Giocondo, and later Antonio da Sangallo the Younger. Upon Raphael's

death, the latter became chief architect, while Peruzzi was named to the position of *Coadjutore*. We can trace the activities of these masters mainly through their drawings.

5. Raphael made unusually careful sketches in preparation for his paintings and as a guide for his assistants.

6. A definite change in the representation of architecture within Raphael's oeuvre corresponds precisely to the transition from a central perspective to an orthogonal section of the interior. A comparison of the Tempietto in *The Marriage of the Virgin* with the hall in *The School of Athens* shows that the centralized building in the earlier painting belongs to the same stage of development as the drawings of the Codex Coner. In both instances the building is presented as seen from far away and, as in the drawings of Bramante's Tempietto, exterior and interior can be taken in at a single glance. On the other hand, the philosophers in *The School of Athens* are gathered within a space that cannot be viewed at a glance, but only through multiple perspective; the distance is so foreshortened and the vault so truncated by the picture's frame that the viewer has the sensation of being drawn into the room,[61] whereas in the case of the Tempietto in *The Marriage of the Virgin* he stands opposite it.[62]

7. The viewer's "correct" vantage point for Bramante's choir of Santa Maria del Popolo lies outside the actual choir, and even in the Tempietto a view of the exterior affords a total view which includes the interior. The Chigi Chapel, seen from the nave or the aisle, provides only a partial view; the correct vantage point lies *within* the room.

Whether Raphael's share in the development of orthogonal projections of interiors can be assessed through autograph drawings is also a question that cannot be answered conclusively. The only truly architectural drawing that traditionally bears Raphael's name, the view of the Pantheon (Uffizi A 164 *verso, recto;* Figs. 25, 26), was included by Fischel in his edition of Raphael's drawings, but with a caveat; Fischel expressed his doubt concerning its authenticity by referring to a very exact copy of it in the Codex Escurialensis.[63] The latter codex was dated by its editor, Egger, to the last decade of the fifteenth century, since one of its drawings bears the date 1491. It is for this reason that Fischel assumed that both the Uffizi drawing and the identical one in the Codex Escurialensis were copied from a common model made before 1500, prior to Raphael's Roman period.[64]

This chain of reasoning, however, is not entirely convincing. It is correct to say that certain views of Rome in the Codex are based on models that reproduce the appearance of the city "prior to the rebuilding undertaken . . . by Alexander VI,"[65] and also that "the year 1491 . . . is the only evidence for a more exact date of the sketchbook."[66] On the other hand, it is common knowledge that it frequently took decades to compile collections of drawings of this kind. Egger assumed that the Codex contains nothing but copies and that we have to "see it as the exercise book of a youthful pupil of Ghirlandaio"; "of course, it is not impossible that [individual] sketches . . . strongly reminiscent of Ridolfo Ghirlandaio . . . were drawn very much later."[67]

With respect to the view of the Pantheon, Egger drew attention to other "thoroughly related drawings, all of which clearly betray their origin from one and the same model, which must have enjoyed a wide reputation at that time."[68] The question of when the model was created brings us back once more to the problem already formulated by Egger: "Why did the model, now presumably lost, become so famous and so frequently copied? The main reason may very well lie in the fact that at the time it was considered a masterpiece of applied perspective and that therefore it was used as an example in the teaching of perspective drawing, just as to this day a representation of the entrance hall of the Pantheon would offer some difficulties because of the short focal point. The same applies to the interior view of the Pantheon . . . The rendering of the interior, the main orders, the upper story, and the base of the dome must have been considered an extraordinary achievement at the time."[69]

The perspective of both views is indeed unusual. In the representation of the interior the vantage point is assumed to lie approximately in the center of the room; a comparison with the section of the same building in the Codex Coner shows that, along with the elimination of the rendering of the bisected outer wall, there is an almost brutal reduction of distance: "As a result they also give a maximum clarity to the relief of the surfaces both of vault and walls as well as to that of the recessed niches."[70] The artist was evidently anxious to show both niches, that of the entrance and of the altar, which were opposite each other. It is a simple matter to solve this problem, if one employs a great enough distance—as does the Codex Coner, by rendering one-half of the building to suggest the way in which a viewer might see it at a glance under the imaginary conditions of the section. Were the artist to stand in the center of the room, however, he could no longer gain that central perspective image of the half of the building which could be considered correct in Alberti's sense. The semicircle between altar and entrance cannot be seen from this point at a single glance.[71] The Uffizi drawing consequently represents the sum total of many glances and is therefore in utter contradiction to Alberti's definition of a perspective view of an interior. It stands, so to speak, halfway between the perspective image of the interior and the orthogonal projection of the inner wall, as defined in Raphael's letter.[72]

The problems inherent in this method are clearly revealed by the fact that the artist makes a factually incorrect rendering of the building by omitting one of the three groups of columns between entrance and altar. He apparently had to reconcile himself to this discrepancy, of which he certainly must have been aware, as being the only way by which he could combine the vantage point within the room—the short distance—with the creation of a fictional image of half the building in perspective. He must have feared that by including the third series of columns he would make the wall too broad and flat, and not sufficiently curved. Geymüller, who published the Pantheon drawing more than a century ago and attributed it to Raphael, seems also to have recognized its purpose and character correctly. The neglect of detail and the omission of the third group of columns led him to assume that "Raphael made these two drawings, or rather these two studies, in connection with the building of St. Peter's. . . . We find it hard to believe that this drawing is related to the restoration of ancient Roman monuments, which occupied him during the last years of his life."[73] For our part, we are inclined to consider the drawings, not as preliminary studies for the basilica itself, but rather as an outgrowth of his preoccupation with the problems of architectural drawing, especially with his rendering of the inner wall. In fact, the surprising number of extant copies tends to prove that the Pantheon drawings were from the very start considered the work of a master, as a paradigm perhaps not so much of applied perspective as of an entirely new method, whose "impossible" perspective, with conscious disregard of traditional precepts, no longer sought to represent the interior as a flat image confronting the viewer, but as a three-dimensional entity that included him. Such an interpretation would also explain the unique position that this drawing occupies; in the vast collection of the Uffizi there is no other drawing of any interior from the first half of the Cinquecento that can compare with this view of the Pantheon.

The attempt to arrive at a new, more correct representation of the inner wall of the Pantheon evidently also led to other experiments. A number of drawings of Italian buildings made by Hermann Vischer the Younger during his journey to Rome in 1514 and 1515 are preserved in the Louvre. One of these (Fig. 27)[74] shows a section of the interior of the Pantheon that, although somewhat awkwardly designed, has all the characteristics of such an experiment. Dated 1515, it represents one of the large niches and the adjacent groups of columns drawn in a plane without perspective. Thus the wall section is represented as if it were part of a straight wall, and the horizontal elements are continued even in places where they do not reflect the moldings of the building, as though the artist were less interested in explaining the building than in the type of construction used in making the drawing. The 1515 date and the peculiar method of representation may well lead to the assumption that in this instance Vischer was merely copying a demonstration drawing by the Raphael group. His elevations of the Cancelleria and of the Farnesina as well as of Bramante's cupola of the Torre Borgia in the Vatican[75] are sufficient evidence that he was familiar with the latest Roman architecture. The German artist, well acquainted with the "Gothic" nonperspective section for architectural drawings practiced in his homeland, was probably less startled by the orthogonal elevation of a wall than were the Italians.[76] On the other hand, another drawing by Vischer in the same collection reveals how little the Pantheon lent itself to representation by means of a "correct" section.

This digression is necessary to gain at least a relative chronology for the views of the Pantheon in the Uffizi and in the Codex Escurialensis. Raphael's letter of 1519, containing his description of the correct orthogonal projection, may well be taken as a *terminus ante quem*. Furthermore, the Pantheon drawing shows the same plurality of vantage points found after 1514 in the studies for St. Peter's by Peruzzi and Giuliano da Sangallo; thus it is more recent, in terms of evolution, than the Bramantesque sections of the Codex Coner with their correct central perspective. For these reasons we are inclined not to date the drawing of the Escurialensis and its models before the second decade of the sixteenth century. This hypothesis permits us to attribute the drawing (Uffizi A 164; Fig. 26) to Raphael, thereby confirming an old tradition, and to regard it as the prototype for the various copies, which unquestionably belong together. Out of all the drawings in this group, only one (Uffizi A 164) comes close to Raphael's drawing style in terms of technique and the execution of the hatching; this sheet alone unites the back and front views that as a rule appear separately. Our relative chronology, taken in conjunction with the start of Raphael's tenure as architect of St. Peter's, would suggest a date around 1514 or 1515; this hypothesis is given added support by the date 1515 on Vischer's drawing.

The Codex Escurialensis contains yet another drawing which may well be a copy after Raphael: a representation of the interior of Santa Costanza (fol. 7; Fig. 28). This drawing shows five arcades projected at short range from far below: the lower halves of the columns are truncated by the edge of the sheet, so that the upper halves appear in "frog perspective." This means that the artist has moved as close to the wall as possible. The effect of an "unrolled" wall is even stronger here than it is in the Pantheon drawing, producing an impression that corresponds exactly to the distorting wide-angle photograph made by a modern camera; the shape of the interior appears elliptic rather than round. Here again the artist resigns himself to these distortions in order to visualize the inner wall and to convey to the viewer the illusion of being surrounded by the walls. With such an advanced use of perspective, which totally neglects the correct *divisiones,* this drawing can hardly have been made before 1500. Once more it is characterized by the experimental qualities of the representational method. The artist tries to find a way by means of which the inner wall can be represented with maximum precision and as large as possible without perspective distortions. For the sake of experimentation he accepts the omission of one range of columns in the interior view of the Pantheon and of the lower halves of the columns in Santa Costanza. Similarly, in the representation of the Pantheon portal (Uffizi A 164 *recto*), only one-half of the lateral columns is shown. The aim of the draftsman of the Codex Coner is to visualize the entire building by bisecting it. In contrast to this, the artist who represented Santa Costanza was concerned solely with the interior, specifically with the space enclosed by the walls.

In his letter, Raphael clearly states the problems posed by interiors such as those of the Pantheon and Santa Costanza when represented by a correct architectural drawing, and with equal clarity he formulates the solution: "And in such drawings, whether the building be round or square, it is not made smaller at the edges in order to make it show two sides. Because the architect cannot take an exact measurement of the reduced line, it is necessary that a device which seeks the actual complete measurements be drawn with parallel lines, not with those that appear equal and yet are not. If the exact measurements of a round form are foreshortened or diminished on the plan, this is quickly discovered in the drawing of the plan, and those things that are foreshortened in the plan, such as domes, arches, triangles, are rendered more perfectly in his direct drawings."[77] This means that the ground plan, elevation, and section of such buildings are in some cases ambiguous by themselves; only a comparison of these three projections can result in a correct image. This interpretation of the architect's drawings is far removed from the point of view held by Alberti, who explains that "the architect has taken from the painter [from his representation in perspective] the finials, the capitals, the base, the columns, the cornices, and all the other admirable features of the building."[78]

The impact of Raphael's 1519 letter to Leo X lies in his systematic separation of ground plan, elevation, and section, well-supported by theory, but also in his definition of the orthogonal projection. It is hard to believe that the ideas he expressed were not also subjected to discussions and practical tests in the *fabbrica* of St. Peter's. We have seen already that Peruzzi and Giuliano da Sangallo availed themselves of the new method, at first in a strange combination with perspective elements. Other studies by Peruzzi made before the sack of Rome likewise betray an intensive interest in the problem of representing an interior view. One of his most famous drawings, the so-called ideal view of St. Peter's (Uffizi A 2; Fig. 29), which according to Frey shows the planning stage around 1515,[79] is most revealing when considered together with the wording of the letter of 1519. The study, drawn in a perspective that also shows the vertical parts step by step, combines elements of ground plan, elevation, and section: ". . . in the foreground only the ground plan is indicated; in the center the elevation up to the height of a horizontal sectional plane, chosen in such a way that the parts lying further back and shown in their full height are nowhere hidden. Only the ground plan is constructed by the perspective vantage-point method; the elevation is drawn as seen . . . but the vanishing points of the diagonals are not adhered to."[80]

The separation of the three views, as recommended by Raphael, is not made here, even though this method also shows the building as bisected. The position of the sectional plane in the center of the arrangement permits a nearly orthogonal representation of the walls, crossing, and transept (but not of the choir and its adjacent chapels). The method, coming close to isometry, was described later at length by Serlio;[81] it forms the basis of the well-known map of Rome, dating from 1564–1565, drawn by Peruzzi's son Sallustio.[82] This method is in fact not suitable for architectural planning for the very reason that the perspective construction is too complex; it serves neither to throw light on the appearance of the interior nor to give the complete measurements to the architect in charge of the building. In both respects the section with the orthogonal projection is far superior.

Still, Peruzzi apparently gave up perspective representations with some reluctance. The new orthogonal projection forced both the artist and the viewer to accept multiple abstractions. One had to imagine a building as bisected and also to renounce the illusion of looking into the bisected building. Now an entirely new relationship had to be established between the image as shown in the drawing and the actual structure, ground plan, and elevation. The new method was simultaneously more professional and less visual; unlike the old method, it could not represent the organic connection between ground plan, exterior, and interior.

It is not surprising that Peruzzi tried over and over again to combine the ground plan and the representation of the interior in the same drawing, and to cling to the practice of drawing in perspective.[83] His ingenious transformation of the section and bird's-eye view (Uffizi A 2; Fig. 29) stands side by side with his study for St. Peter's (Uffizi A 107; Fig. 30),[84] which includes a section of the dome area reduced to much smaller scale in the center of the ground plan of the four main piers. "The cross-section is not drawn as the central portion of a great church, nor even as an isolated chapel, as it seems at first sight, but as a scene such as one would view when standing in the center of the space: a painter's concept of architecture."[85] As in the view of the Pantheon and in Peruzzi's project for St. Peter's, the vantage point is assumed to be the center of the domed interior. Peruzzi ignores both the separation of the three views prescribed by Raphael and the uniformity of scale. When, as in this instance, he wishes to give a quick visualization of an architectural idea, he chooses the older method of mixed representation. Unlike the separate orthogonal elevations, this has the advantage of permitting one to visualize the project literally at one glance.

A drawing preserved in Munich, possibly by an artist of the Sangallo circle and showing a view of Bramante's San Biagio alla Pagnotta (Fig. 31), provides an interesting example of how the same method was utilized by another architect of Peruzzi's generation. Like Peruzzi's study, this sketch gives fairly accurate measurements; similarly, a perspective view of the interior is included in the ground plan of the domed part. Yet in contrast to Peruzzi, whose drawing contains almost no perspective elements and thus approaches an orthogonal projection, this artist still uses a high horizon in the earlier manner.[86]

The body of extant drawings suggests that Antonio da Sangallo the Younger, Raphael's youngest colleague at St. Peter's, was the first to make consistent use of the correct orthogonal projection when representing an interior by means of a section (Figs. 32, 33). Sangallo, in his capacity of *Coadjutore,* was Raphael's right-hand man at the *fabbrica* during the last years of the latter's life. These were the years in which Raphael was engaged in making drawings of ancient Rome; along with the method of actual representation, they formed the subject of his letter to Leo X.

Even before his appointment as *Coadjutore,* Sangallo had been working at St. Peter's in the capacities of *faber lignarius* and *carpentarius.*[87] He was the only important Roman architect during the Renaissance who rose from the ranks of craftsmen.[88] Unlike Bramante, Raphael, and Peruzzi, all of whom began as painters, Sangallo had not learned perspective drawing as part of his professional training. He was more receptive, therefore, to Raphael's new ideas than was Peruzzi, who was about the same age. Perhaps it was for this reason that Sangallo was proposed for the position of *Coadjutore* by Raphael. Peruzzi, the painter, may have looked on the orthogonal projection as offering less with respect to visualization, but Sangallo, the craftsman, must have recognized its advantages of greater clarity and readability. He must have welcomed it also as a final solution to the problem of representing an interior by means of a drawing and therefore adhered to it consistently, while the more introspective Peruzzi, "with his strong theoretical tendencies and talents,"[89] attempted to reconcile the advantages of the richer, more visual, and painterlike perspective representation of an interior with those of an orthogonal projection.

In my opinion it is most probable that Sangallo, as Raphael's assistant, cooperated in developing the orthogonal projection. By 1520, his knowledge and ability as a draftsman must have been recognized. In accordance with contemporary usage, his promotion to the position of chief architect of St. Peter's was based more on his mastery of architectural drawing than on his practical experience in building. Nothing is known about Sangallo's activities as an artist prior to his appointment in 1516. "None of his nearly one thousand architectural drawings in the Uffizi can be dated with certainty before 1517 or 1518."[90] His productivity thus falls in the years during which he was Raphael's assistant at the *fabbrica.*

Antonio da Sangallo may be considered to have developed the genre of the architect's drawings in the narrower sense, as defined by Raphael's letter. It is true that three separate views of one building occur already in the Codex Coner—those of the Tempietto, which is shown in its ground plan, exterior, and section. The two latter views, however, are shown in perspective; only the orthogonal projection makes it possible "to understand all of the measurements and to know how to find all of the parts of a building without error." The orthogonal method is at once more professional and less visual. Ever since its introduction, the architect's manner of seeing and representing has deviated from that of the painter, and the unity between the two arts, which Alberti had established in principle and which Bramante had put into practice, has dissolved.

This process coincides exactly with the separation of the two professions, which became increasingly evident in the first half of the sixteenth century. Sangallo was not only the first chief architect of St. Peter's to come from the building crafts, he was also the first to work exclusively as an architect.[91]

The orthogonal and perspective image of an interior were used side by side until the end of the eighteenth century. Peruzzi's perspective construction became widely known through Serlio's *Treatise* and is encountered again in the oeuvre of Androuet Du Cerceau, and later in that of Fischer von Erlach, for example. It is not by chance that this manner of representation came to be known as cavalier projection since it was always concerned with picturelike visualization and not with the working drawing.

The orthogonal projection became more generally known through the engravings of Sangallo's pupil, Antonio Labacco, who reproduced Sangallo's St. Peter's project (before 1549) by means of section and elevation. Palladio, who in other ways also had much in common with Antonio da Sangallo, always employed the orthogonal section. Above all his *Quattro Libri* established the orthogonal view as the more professional representation, indispensable for the realization of the actual building.[92] But only in the Quattrocento and in the first two decades of the Cinquecento, in an age that considered the "mathematical perspective [of a picture] not only as a guarantee of its correctness, but perhaps even more of its esthetic fulfillment,"[93] could the method of drawing an interior become an artistic problem of such magnitude. Only in this period did the change in method herald a changing concept of space.

Notes

1. Concerning the transalpine renderings and elevations, see for instance O. Kletzl, and B. Grimschitz, *Hanns Puchspaum* (Vienna, 1947).

2. See E. Panofsky, "Die Perspective als symbolische Form," in *Vorträge der Bibliothek Warburg* (1924/25), pp. 264ff.; idem, *The Codex Huygens and Leonardo da Vinci's Art Theory* (London, 1940), pp. 160ff. (hereafter Panofsky, *Codex Huygens*); also J. White, "Developments in Renaissance Perspective," *Journal of the Warburg and Courtauld Institutes* 12 (1949): pp. 58ff. (hereafter White, "Developments").

3. Alberti, *Architettura* II: 1.

4. Alberti explains the theory of perspective as it applies to painting in his treatise *On Painting* (passim), which was written before his *Ten Books on Architecture.* Hence, knowledge of it is taken for granted in the latter essay. His distinction between drawings of painters and of architects departs from the Gothic tradition only in theory but not in practice. Villard de Honnecourt had already used both perspective and shading in his view of the interior of Reims cathedral; see H. R. Hahnloser, *Villard de Honnecourt* (Vienna, 1935), p. 162 and pl. 60. Villard's sketch is probably intended to produce a visual impression in the manner of a painter rather than to serve as an actual working drawing.

5. See H. Siebenhüner, *Deutsche Künstler am Mailänder Dom* (Munich, 1944), p. 17. Measurements are entered in Bolognese feet on the ground plan and in Milanese feet on the elevation.

6. See Otto Kletzl, *Planfragmente,* p. 19.

7. *Ibid.,* p. 18.

8. Alberti, *Architettura* II: 1.

9. See Robert Oertel, "Wandmalerei," pp. 259ff., as well as the examples listed in L. H. Heydenreich, *Reallexikon zur Deutschen Kunstgeschichte* 1 (1937): col. 925. For a late example, referred to in a letter of Alberto Pio dated 9 March 1515, concerning the cathedral of his home town of Carpi: "I shall soon send the model, which is finished . . . A. soon as it is here, I can begin to work" (see H. Semper, F. O. Schulze, and W. Barth, *Capri, ein Fürstensitz der Renaissance* [Dresden, 1882], p. 53). The model was to be transported by mules, which gives some general idea of its size.

10. Antonio Manetti, *Brunelleschi,* E. Toesca, ed. (1927), pp. 78ff. In his description of a technical process, Manetti can hardly be accused of idolizing Brunelleschi, as was his tendency.

11. *Ibid.*

12. *Ibid.,* p. 79.

13. *Ibid.*

14. Reproduced in J. Meder, *Die Handzeichnung* (Vienna, 1923), Fig. 293.

15. Alberti, *Pittura* I: 29.

16. Cod. Vat. Barb. Lat. 4424, fol. 28; see C. Huelsen, *Il libro di G. da Sangallo,* pp. xxix, 39; and Fabriczy, *Handzeichnungen,* passim.

17. See note 4.

18. See V. Golubew, *Die Skizzenbücher Jacopo Bellinis* (Brussels, 1908–12), London, fol. 55b, 67a; Paris, fol. 27a.

19. In addition to these stone buildings

there are also wooden frame constructions, which are basically similar: see, for example, *ibid.*, London, fol. 59b, 99b; Paris, fol. 31a, 33a.

20. *Ibid.*, fol. 69.

21. *Treatise*, J. R. Spencer, ed. (1965), I: p. 22, fol. 11 *recto*.

22. *Ibid.*, I: pp. 303ff., fol. 177 *verso* ff.

23. Written before 1465, with a dedication to Piero di Cosimo; see W. von Oettingen, ed., *A. Averlino Filaretes Traktat über die Baukunst* (Vienna, 1890), pp. 6, 9: according to Oettingen, the drawings are not by Filarete.

24. Biblioteca Nazionale, Cod. Magl. 17: 1, 30, fol. 169. See also Filarete, I: fol. 144 *recto*.

25. Quoted from a copy of the Cod. Magl. in the Avery Library, Columbia University, New York.

26. Biblioteca Nazionale, Cod. Magl. 17: 1, 30, fol. 75. See also Filarete, I: fol. 70 *verso*. Evidently the architecture of the loggia was inspired by the Ospedale degli Innocenti. It is, therefore, quite reasonable to consider the little sketch in the *Treatise* as a copy of Brunelleschi's design for the orphanage, which, according to the explicit testimony of Manetti, was still preserved in the second half of the Cinquecento.

27. See L. Grassi, "Disegni inediti di Simone del Pollaiolo detto il Cronaca," *Palladio* 7 (1943): pp. 14–22.

28. See Heydenreich, *Leonardo*, p. 89.

29. *Ibid.*, Fig. 116.

30. For example, in Ms. B, fol. 16 *recto* (see Heydenreich, *Leonardo*, Fig. 119).

31. Taken from R. Papini, *Francesco di Giorgio, Architetto* (Florence, 1946), p. 2: Fig. 13.

32. See note 10.

33. See Thomas Ashby, "Drawings," passim; G. de Angelis d'Ossat, "L'autore del Codice Londinese attribuito ad A. Coner," *Palladio* n.s.1 (1951): pp. 84–94. The latter author considers the older handwriting of the codex (which is all that concerns us here) as that of Giovanni Battista da Sangallo, known as Il Gobbo, who drew "as though he had listened to Bramante and his followers." The drawings in London evidently are copies; their date of execution need not be of concern here. I agree with the date suggested by d'Ossat for the originals used by the copyist.

34. Alberti, *Pittura* I: 20.

35. H. Kauffmann, "Über 'Rinascere', 'Rinascita' und einige Stilmerkmale der Quattrocento-baukunst: Analyse der Raumgestaltung Brunelleschis," in *Concordia Decennalis* (1943), pp. 134ff. (hereafter, Kauffmann, "Analyse").

36. See, among others, the examples cited by Oertel, "Wandmalerei," pp. 259ff. Another instance of a drawing made by a painter specifically for an architectural project is Mantegna's *mirabile disegno* of 1472 for the courtyard of the castle of San Giorgio in Mantua; see C. Cottafavi, *Ricordi e Documenti sulla costruzione del Palazzo Ducale di Mantova* (Mantua, 1939), p. 34; W. Lotz, Review of Cottafavi in *Zeitschrift für Kunstgeschichte* 10 (1941/42): pp. 228ff. Since the "painter was considered a specialist for architectural planning" (Oertel, "Wandmalerei," p. 268), the lack of Italian

architects' drawings in the narrow sense is hardly accidental. On the contrary, one is tempted to inquire whether such a category of drawings ever existed. The fact that the model played a much greater role in the South than in the North has a close bearing on the question. Ackerman comes to very similar conclusions, "Architectural Practice," passim.

37. See Oertel, "Wandmalerei," passim.

38. Alberti, *Pittura* II: 38; Kauffmann, "Analyse," pp. 134ff., recognized the significance of this passage for the design of facades in the Quattrocento.

39. Alberti, *Pittura* I: 20.

40. Ackerman has shown that the design of the Belvedere courtyard in the Vatican is calculated for being seen from the windows of the *stanze* (*Belvedere*, passim). Another example of the method is the drawing of the interior of S. Biagio alla Pagnotta (Fig. 31).

41. Edited by G. Mongeri under the title, *Le Rovine di Roma al principio del secolo XVI* (Milan, 1875). (Hereafter, Mongeri, *Rovine*.)

42. See K. Feuchtmayr, *Die Bildhauer der Fuggerkapelle bei St. Anna zu Augsburg* (Munich, 1952), pp. 10ff.; also W. Lotz, *Plan und Bauwerk*, pp. 20, 24, Fig. 8.

43. At about the same time a master from the circle of Altdorfer created some impressive interiors; see P. Halm, "Eine Gruppe von Architekturzeichnungen aus dem Umkreis A. Altdorfer," *Münchner Jahrbuch der Bildenden Kunst* 2 (1951): pp. 127ff.; Halm correctly points out that ". . . only in the Danube school . . . did the representation of the interior reach such importance and

such a degree of independence in the first decades [of the sixteenth century]. Unlike his Italian contemporaries, the creator of these drawings did not have to cope with the problem of mathematically correct perspective, a heritage that the early sixteenth century had received in the South from the Quattrocento.

44. Dagobert Frey, *St. Peter—Entwurf*, passim. This work still contains the best survey of the problems concerning the drawings for St. Peter's.

45. See N. Ferri, *Indice geografico dei disegni di architettura e pittura nella R. Galleria degli Uffizi* (Rome, 1885), pp. 203, 217; and C. von Fabriczy, *Handzeichnungen*, p. 96. Fabriczy considers the unusually large sheet—74.5 × 44 cm.—as a "reconstruction"—in the form of a section—of the conversion of the main room of the Diocletian *thermae* into a church, Santa Maria degli Angeli; see also G. Marchini, *Giuliano da Sangallo* (Florence, 1942), p. 102, who speaks of an "ideally completed section of the Diocletian *thermae*." However, it might be difficult to reconcile the drawn-in altar and the apostles' statues in the niches of the high wall with this identification, particularly since there are hardly any contemporaneous analogies one might cite. The sheet carries on the verso the notation *tempio grecho*, in what Fabriczy takes to be Sangallo's handwriting, while according to Marchini the style of the drawing and the inscription point to his workshop. Yet ". . . cooperative practices within the Sangallo shop were such that a notation by one person does not rule out the attribution of a drawing to someone else" (Degenhart, "Dante, Leonardo und Sangallo," p. 194). The drawing in question is closely related to

Peruzzi's study for St. Peter's (Uffizi A 161; our Fig. 20). Nothing has come down to us from the early sixteenth century about projects dealing with the conversion of the Diocletian *thermae* into a church. And Michelangelo's Santa Maria degli Angeli was the result of a new plan, which was not given consideration until after the middle of the Cinquecento. Therefore, there can be no reservations in describing the drawing as a plan for St. Peter's, made by Giuliano during the last years of his life, at a time when planning activity was focused on the nave and its connection with the domed interior. This would not overrule Marchini's objections based on the style of the sheet. The architecture represented shows the characteristics of Giuliano's late style; and of all the masters who might be considered, only he is the most likely candidate. It is possible, although in my opinion not probable, that it was made by a member of the workshop under Giuliano's supervision.

46. See note 16.

47. Fol. 30 *recto* (see Fabriczy, *Handzeichnungen,* p. 44).

48. Huelsen, *Il Libro di G. da Sangallo,* speaking of "many arbitrary restorations" (text p. 54), fails to understand the principle of representation.

49. The earliest date given to the Codex Barberini is the 1465 one inscribed on the title page; the latest entries are by Francesco da Sangallo and were drawn by him after the death of his father Giuliano. Only a few of the drawings can be dated accurately, none of which are of concern here. The present author is well aware of the hypothetical nature of the relative chronology attempted. The fact that Huelsen often proposes similar dates on the basis of quite different criteria (*ibid.,* pp. xxvff.) and that none of his dates contradict our chronology may lend some support to our grouping of the drawings.

50. See Fabriczy, *Handzeichnungen,* p. 58.

51. Degenhart has pointed out Giuliano's adaptability and susceptibility to outside influences. Giuliano's late designs for the facade of San Lorenzo in Florence show how the septuagenarian adopted the classic style of the circle of Bramante and Raphael.

52. The letter is reprinted in its entirety in Vincenzo Golzio, *Raffaello,* pp. 78ff.; see also J. Vogel, *Bramante und Raffael* (Leipzig, 1910).

53. Jakob Burckhardt, *Die Kunst der Renaissance in Italien* (Stuttgart, 1932), 6: p. 27.

54. Golzio, *Raffaello,* p. 89.

55. *Ibid.* The definition of the exterior wall given here may be considered an innovation, at least so far as theory is concerned, and possibly even with respect to its practical implementation. Several drawings of facades which can be dated around 1500—and especially the Lombard, Bramantesque sheets of this kind—reproduce such details as portals or windows in perspective; in some instances one even looks into the interior of the building through the open portal. See, for example: Giuliano da Sangallo, Uffizi A 279—illustrated in Giuseppe Marchini, *Sangallo,* pl. 23b; sketchbook of "Bramantino," fol. 14—reproduced in Mongeri, *Rovine,* pl. 14; design for Santa Maria presso San Celso in Milan (?) by Cesare Cesarino, Louvre—illustrated in C. Baroni, *L'Architettura Lombarda dal Bramante al Richini* (Milan, 1941), Fig. 89; and Cesa-

riano's (?) project for the facade of Santa Maria presso San Satiro—in Giovannoni, *Saggi,* p. 73.

56. Golzio, *Raffaello,* p. 90.

57. Kauffmann, "Analyse," p. 140; quoted here in a positive way, whereas Kauffmann means it negatively to show what qualities are lacking in Quattrocento examples.

58. The building itself made little progress under Leo X.

59. Raphael, too, ordered a preliminary model of the projected basilica to be made (see his letter to Baldassare Castiglione, dated 1514, written immediately after his assumption of responsibility for the building, Golzio, *Raffaello,* p. 30).

60. From Frey, *St. Peter-Entwurf,* p. 70.

61. The fresco shows only the inner wall, one can question the usefulness of reconstructing the exterior of the building; see C. Huelsen, "Die Halle in Raffaels *Schule von Athen,*" *Mitteilungen des Kunsthistorischen Instituts in Florenz* 1 (1911): pp. 229ff. According to Raphael's letter, the relation of interior and exterior can be understood only if the ground plan and the exterior wall are treated in separate drawings. Since this was obviously not the case in *The School of Athens,* the viewer neither can nor shall form an idea of the building exterior.

62. There was no iconographic necessity to represent *The Marriage of the Virgin* in front of the building (see, for instance, Giotto in the Arena Chapel, Padua; Masolino, Castiglion d'Olona; and even Ghirlandaio in Santa Maria Novella, Florence).

63. *Raffaels Zeichnungen* (Berlin, 1913–41), 5: pls. 216, 217, and text.

64. The connection with the Pantheon view had been recognized by Hermann Egger, *Codex Escurialensis,* text, pp. 37, 93. He also provided a listing of the various copies—views of the interior: Uffizi A 164 *verso* (reproduced in H. von Geymüller, *Projects,* pl. 44); Uffizi A 1950 ("Jacopo Sansovino"); Codex Escurialensis, fol. 30—views of the portal in the portico: Uffizi A 164 *recto,* (illustrated in: H. von Geymüller, *Raffaello Sanzio studiato come Architetto* [Milan, 1884], pl. 2, and Fischel. *Raffaels Zeichnungen,* 5: pl. 217); Uffizi A 1948 *verso* and A 1949 ("Jacopo Sansovino." Uffizi A 681, by Sallustio Peruzzi may also be based on the same model); Codex Escurialensis, fol. 29 *verso;* London, Sir John Soane Museum, vol. Margeret Chinnery, fol. 6 (once owned by Vasari, as is indicated by the ornamentation on the reverse side, a fact which, to the best of our knowledge, has never been noted in the literature). Compared with Uffizi A 164 the two folios in the Codex Escurialensis are clearly weaker, details of the model are misunderstood, and the visible area is smaller. In view of the special character of the perspective, all this can be attributed to the lack of confidence of the copyist.

65. Egger, *Codex Escurialensis,* text, p. 54.

66. *Ibid.,* text, p. 46.

67. *Ibid.*

68. See note 64.

69. Egger, *Codex Escurialensis,* text, pp. 37ff. The choice, by no means self-evident, of a vantage point within the entrance hall appears to be more important than the difficulty of the representation. This applies equally to the interior view. The exterior

views of the Codex Coner choose a vantage point outside of the building; in the representation of the portal even the entrance hall is cut off from view.

70. White, "Developments," p. 54.

71. As it is "that part of the monument . . . which is found to be too wide to be taken in at one glance" (H. von Geymüller, "Trois dessins d'architecture inédits de Raphael," *Gazette des Beaux Arts* 3 [1870]: p. 80; hereafter, Geymüller, "Dessins").

72. Orthogonal projection might also be described as perspective with an unlimited number of vantage points.

73. Geymüller, "Dessins," pp. 80ff.

74. See L. Demonts, *Inventaire Général des Dessins des Ecoles du Nord, Ecoles allemande et suisse* (Paris, 1938), 2: pp. 71ff. and #335 *verso*.

75. Regarding the drawing of the *Torre Borgia*, see Ackerman, *Belvedere*, p. 193, as well as the illustration in Demonts, *Inventaire*, #335 *verso* (who describes it as a kind of Bramantesque Tempietto). For the Vischer drawings mentioned hereafter, see *ibid.*, passim.

76. The present author knows of no other orthogonal representation of the Pantheon dating from the Cinquecento. The detailed study, showing a window and rafters of the upper story, published by G. Zorzi as one of the "Due schizzi archeologici di Raffaello fra i disegni Palladiani di Londra," *Palladio* n. s. 2 (1952): p. 171, characteristically mixes perspective and orthogonal projection.

77. Golzio, *Raffaello*, p. 90. I agree with Vogel (see note 52) that the subse-

quent description of perspective, found only in the Munich copy of the letter and written in a different hand, must be an addendum not authored by Raphael.

78. Alberti, *Pittura* II: 38.

79. See Frey, *St. Peter-Entwurf*, pp. 28 f. and pl. 3.

80. *Ibid.*, p. 29.

81. *Ibid.* for the Serlio references.

82. See E. Rocchi, *Le Piante iconografiche e prospettiche di Roma del secolo XVI* (Rome, 1902), p. 108; Frey, *St. Peter-Entwurf*, p. 48; and Lotz, *Plan und Bauwerk*, p. 14 and Fig. 4.

83. See also the design for San Petronio, Bologna, datable to 1522 and preserved in the church's museum—illustrated in Venturi, *Storia* 11/1: Fig. 360; it represents the cupola and the adjacent bay of the nave in a perspective section with a high horizon, whereas in the view of the broken-up choir chapel even parts of the exterior are visible.

84. See Frey, *St. Peter-Entwurf*, p. 28, and Ackerman, "Architectural Principles," p. 9 and Fig. 8.

85. See Ackerman, "Architectural Principles," p. 9.

86. A few typical examples only from Peruzzi's large drawing oeuvre are mentioned here. See also the illustrations in Geymüller, "Dessins," and Frey, *St. Peter-Entwurf*, passim. The present author, in contrast to Frey, *ibid.*, pp. 48ff. and to his own earlier statement in *Plan und Bauwerk*, p. 17 and Fig. 4, sees no reason to deny Baldassare Peruzzi's authorship of Uffizi A 23 *verso*, an important and, in our context, very significant study for St. Peter's. Be-

cause of the appearance of the single cupola, it must represent an early planning stage.

87. See Ackerman, "Architectural Principles," p. 10.

88. *Ibid.*

89. Frey, *St. Peter-Entwurf*, p. 37.

90. Ackerman, *Belvedere*, p. 49.

91. Benvenuto Cellini's opinion of Sangallo shows that the latter's career appeared to be rather extraordinary to his contemporaries ". . . by not having been either a sculptor or a painter rather, on the contrary, only a master carpenter; nevertheless one can see a certain noble virtue in his architectural works" (*Ricordi, Prose e Poesie di Benvenuto Cellini,* F. Tassi, ed. [Florence, 1829], 3: p. 367). For Peruzzi's alleged opinion of Vitruvius, "seeing that he was neither painter nor sculptor, which thing made him ignorant of the most beautiful of this admirable art [architecture]," see *ibid.,* p. 369.

92. "In fact Palladio, as is shown by the examination of all of the signed drawings preserved in London, has never represented buildings in perspective, rather only in geometrical projection, not only when he rendered the main views but also the interior and lateral walls" (G. Zorzi, "Alcuni disegni di Falconetto," *Palladio,* n. s. 5 [1955]: p. 31).

93. Panofsky, *Codex Huygens,* p. 160.

Postscript

For the analysis of Alberti's text on architectural drawings and models I used Cosimo Bartoli's Italian translation of *De re aedificatoria* (Florence, 1550; republished by Stefano Ticozzi in the Raccolta dei Classici Italiani, Milan, 1833). As Howard Saalman rightly observed, I had not noticed that Bartoli left out a crucial portion of Alberti's Latin sentence: after describing the difference between the painter's and the architect's drawing, Alberti continues that "the architect . . . renders the relief [of the architectural members] by drawing the ground plan, and he renders in other drawings the shape and the extension of every facade and every flank, using the correct angles and the unaltered lines . . ." (See H. Saalman, "Early Renaissance Architectural Theory and Practice in Antonio Filarete's *Trattato di Architettura,*" in *The Art Bulletin,* 41 (1959), pp. 89ff.; for the Latin text see ibid., p. 105, note 21 and the recent edition of *De re aedificatoria* in Giovanni Orlandi, *Leon Battista Alberti: L'Architettura* [Milan, 1966], pp. 98ff.). Saalman also points out that the "letter of 1519 to Leo X, almost surely by Raphael, is, after all, nothing else than (in contrast to Bartoli!) a *correct* translation and interpretation of the Alberti passage, made by a man for whom the problem of developing more effectual means of architectural representation to meet the needs of a changing architecture was no longer a matter of theoretical interest but of pressing everyday necessity on the building of new Saint Peter's. Alberti was, as usual, fifty years ahead of his time" (p. 105f.). For Alberti's method of planning and drawing, see now also the excellent study of Eugenio Battisti, "Il metodo progettuale secondo il *De re aedificatoria*," in *Il Sant'Andrea di Mantova e Leon Battista Alberti: Atti del Convegno di studi nel quinto centenario della basilica di Sant'Andrea* (Mantova, 1972 [1975]), pp. 131ff.

Howard Saalman has recently re-edited Manetti's *Life of Brunelleschi*, adding an English translation (University Park and London, 1970).

For Filarete's treatise see now *Antonio Averlino detto il Filarete: Trattato di Architettura*, A. M. Finoli and L. Grassi eds. (Milan, 1972).

For the authorship of the Codex Coner, see the important study by Tilmann Buddensieg, "Bernardo della Volpaia und Giovanni Francesco da Sangallo: Der Autor des Codex Coner und seine Stellung im Sangallos-Kreis," in *Römisches Jahrbuch für Kunstgeschichte*, 15 (1975): pp. 89ff. According to Buddensieg, the draftsman, Bernardo della Volpaia, was at least forty years old when the Codex was given its final shape around 1515. In all probability, the sketchbook is not the product of a young man in the Sangallo circle, but rather represents the sum of experience of an artist who could look back to twenty years of measuring and surveying ancient and modern architecture.

For Hermann Vischer's architectural drawings see my article "Zu Hermann Vischer's d. J. Aufnahmen italienischer Bauten." in *Miscellanea Bibliothecae Hertzianae* (Munich, 1961), pp. 167ff.; and Eugenio Battisti's study in *Il Sant'Andrea di Mantova*.

For Raphael's letter to Leo, see also *Raffaello Sanzio, Tutti gli Scritti,* E. Camesasca ed. (Milan, 1956), pp. 57ff; for the problem of authorship pp. 44ff., and Vincenzo Fontana and Paolo Morachiello, "Vitruvio e Raffaello, il *De architettura* di Vitruvio nella traduzione inedita di Fabio Calvo Ravennate" (Rome, 1975), pp. 26ff. The letter is also discussed by Stefano Ray, *Raffaello architetto* (Bari, 1974), pp. 362ff. The drawing Uffizi A 20, which I tentatively dated after 1513 and connected with the method of rendering described in Raphael's letter, has been attributed subsequently to an "artist of the Sangallo circle under the decisive influence of Bramante" by Count Metternich (Franz Graf Wolff Metternich, *Die Erbauung der Peterskirche in Rom im 16. Jahrhundert* (Vienna, 1972), 2 vols.: 1, p. 37). Metternich demonstrates that the variant for the piers under the dome shown on the sheet must have been discarded when the piers were begun in 1506. Thus the drawing would predate the beginning of work on them. But could it not show the early planning stage and still have been done by a draftsman who was interested in recording the planning and building history for didactic purposes? When discussing the drawing Uffizi A 164 and its relation to the pertinent sheet in the Codex Escurialensis, I did not realize that the passage of Raphael's letter, which describes the orthogonal elevation, is practically identical to the text of Alberti's *De re aedificatoria,* as I have mentioned above. Furthermore, Hanno-Walter Kruft has shown that the Codex Escurialensis was in Spain from 1509 on ("Concerning the Date of the Codex Escurialensis," *Burlington Magazine,* 122 (1970): pp. 44ff.). Consequently, the method of representation used for the interior of the Pantheon in Uffizi A 164 is not as unusual as I thought; and the latest possible date for the interior view of the Pantheon in Codex Escurialensis fol. 30 (which is closely connected to Uffizi A 164) is 1508, the year in which Raphael began working in Rome. Thus the problem of Uffizi A 164 will have to be reconsidered. It would seem plausible that Oskar Fischel was right in assuming that both the Uffizi and the Escurialensis sheets are copies after a lost prototype. While this does not exclude the attribution of Uffizi A 164 to Raphael, it would appear improbable that Raphael invented this rendering of the interior of the Pantheon.

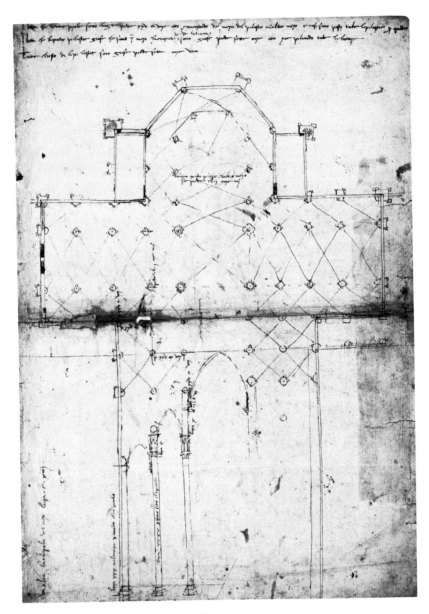

1. Andrea de' Vincenti (?), 1389, Milan
Cathedral; Bologna, San Petronio
(photo: Bibliotheca Hertziana)

2. Pisanello, drawing of an interior,
Paris, Louvre (photo: Bernhard
Degenhart)

3. Giuliano da Sangallo, Hagia Sophia;
Rome, Biblioteca Vaticana, Cod. Lat.
Barb. 4424, fol. 28 (photo: Bernhard
Degenhart)

4. Filarete, House of Virtues; Florence,
Biblioteca Nazionale, Cod. Magl. XVII,
1, 30, fol. 169 (photo: Rome, Gab. Fot.
Naz.)

5. Filarete, *Treatise on Architecture,*
Marketplace; Florence, Biblioteca
Nazionale, Cod. Magl. XVII, 1, 30, fol.
75 (photo: Bib. Naz.)

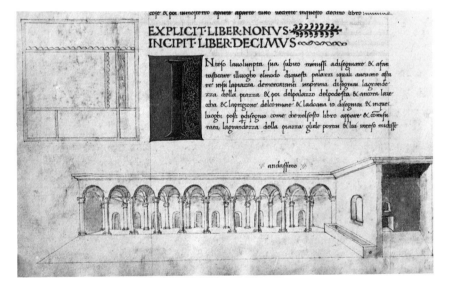

6. Cronaca, nave of Santissimi Apostoli;
Florence, privately owned

7. Leonardo da Vinci, study for a centralized building; Milan, Biblioteca
Ambrosiana, Cod. Atl., fol. 205 *verso*
(photo: Bib. Am.)

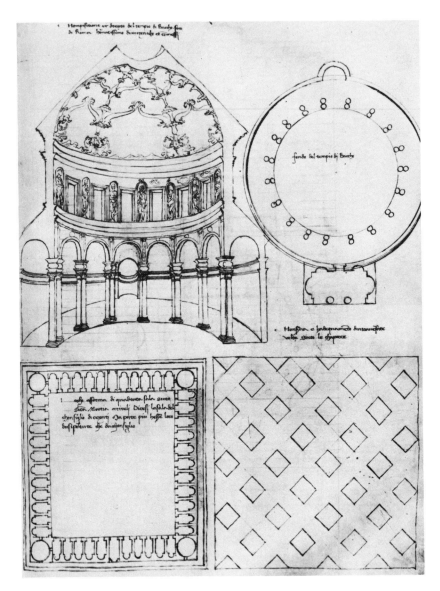

8. Francesco di Giorgio Martini, Santa
Costanza; Turin, Biblioteca ex-Reale
(photo: Bibliotheca Hertziana)

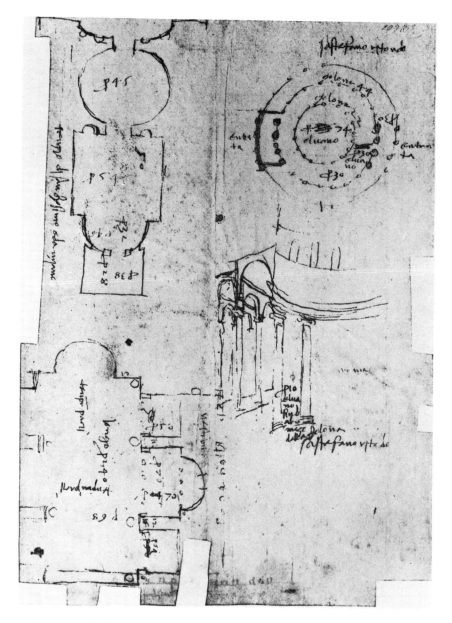

9. Francesco di Giorgio Martini, Santo
Stefano Rotondo; Uffizi A 330, Florence
(photo: Bibliotheca Hertziana)

49

11. Codex Coner, Tempietto, San Pietro in Montorio; London, Sir John Soane Museum, fol. 33 (photo: London, Cooper)

10. Codex Coner, Tempietto, San Pietro in Montorio; London, Sir John Soane Museum, fol. 34 (photo: London, Cooper)

13. Codex Coner, Pantheon; London, Sir John Soane Museum, fol. 36 (photo: London, Cooper)

12. Codex Coner, Pantheon; London, Sir John Soane Museum, fol. 35 (photo: London, Cooper)

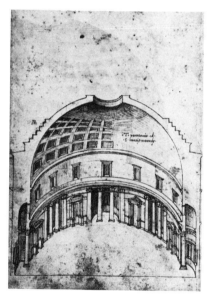

14. Milan, Santa Maria presso San
Satiro, choir (photo: Milan, Crimmella)

15. Rome, Santa Maria del Popolo, choir (photo: Rome, Gab. Fot. Naz.)

16. Codex Coner, Basilica of Maxentius; London, Sir John Soane Museum, fol. 59 (photo: London, Cooper)

Templi pacis·

17. "Bramantino," antique interior;
Milan, Biblioteca Ambrosiana (photo:
Bib. Am.)

18. "Bramantino," antique interior with
plan; Milan, Biblioteca Ambrosiana
(photo: Bib. Am.)

19. Sebastian Loscher, Fugger chapel in
St. Anna's, Augsburg; Städtische
Kunstsammlungen (photo: Munich,
Hirmer)

55

20. Baldassare Peruzzi, project for St.
Peter's; Florence, Uffizi A 161 (photo:
Florence, Gab. Fot. Sopr.)

21. Giuliano da Sangallo, project for
St. Peter's; Florence, Uffizi A 131 (photo:
Florence, Gab. Fot. Sopr.)

22. Giuliano da Sangallo, Minerva
Medica; Biblioteca Vaticana, Cod. Lat.
Barb. 4424, fol. 6 (photo: Gab. Fot.
Vat.)

23. Giuliano da Sangallo, antique
circular temples; Rome, Biblioteca
Vaticana, Cod. Lat. Barb. 4424, fol. 37
(photo: Gab. Fot. Vat.)

24. Giuliano da Sangallo, project for a
centralized building; Rome, Biblioteca
Vaticana, Cod. Lat. Barb. 4424, fol. 59
verso (photo: Gab. Fot. Vat.)

25. Raphael (?), Pantheon; Florence,
Uffizi A 164 *verso* (photo: Florence,
Gab. Fot. Sopr.)

26. Raphael (?), Pantheon; Florence,
Uffizi A 164 *recto* (photo: Florence,
Gab. Fot. Sopr.)

27. Hermann Vischer, 1515, Pantheon;
Paris, Louvre (photo: Munich, P. Halm)

28. Codex Escorialensis, Santa Costanza, fol. 7

29. Baldassare Peruzzi, project for St. Peter's; Florence, Uffizi A 2 (photo: Florence, Gab. Fot. Sopr.)

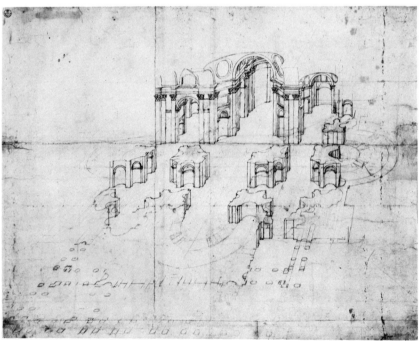

30. Baldassare Peruzzi, project for St.
Peter's; Florence, Uffizi A 107 (photo:
Florence, Gab. Fot. Sopr.)

31. Circle of Antonio da Sangallo the
Younger, San Biagio alla Pagnotta;
Munich, Staatliche Graphische Samm-
lung (photo: Munich, Staat. Graph.
Sammlung)

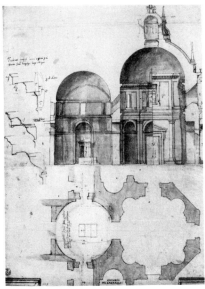

32. Antonio da Sangallo the Younger,
project for St. Peter's; Florence, Uffizi
A 66 (photo: Florence, Gab. Fot. Sopr.)

33. Antonio da Sangallo the Younger,
project for a centralized building;
Florence, Uffizi A 173 (photo: Florence,
Gab. Fot. Sopr.)

2
NOTES ON THE CENTRALIZED CHURCH OF THE RENAISSANCE

One of the distinguishing characteristics of Italian Renaissance architecture, as Jakob Burckhardt pointed out, is the preference for churches built on a centralized plan. Rudolf Wittkower has in an exemplary study of the phenomenon, examined the theological and philosophical attitudes that lie behind the way centralized buildings were interpreted and used in Renaissance architectural theory and practice. The plans of these buildings are either circular or have certain affinities with the circle. Wittkower demonstrated that the circle was regarded as the perfect geometric form, the absolute harmony of which was equated with the perfection of God. This concept, ultimately derived from Plato's Timaeus, was embodied in numerous buildings erected in the fifteenth and sixteenth centuries.[1]

The symbolic meaning of the circle applied only to a limited extent to centralized buildings in the form of a polygon or Greek cross. Therefore the centralized plan must have had other inherent qualities that were responsible for its frequent appearance during the Renaissance. One of these is surely that it is a monument or "memorial" in quite a different sense than the traditional longitudinal building. Centralized churches of the Renaissance have certain features that medieval sacral buildings lack, even when they are built on a centralized plan. As a rule the Renaissance churches are freestanding, and look virtually identical, or at least very similar, on all sides. Furthermore, they are so constructed that their highest point, the tip of the monument so to speak, rises over the center of the building; the center is covered by a dome.

The conception of the church as a monument in the traditional sense of the term seems to make its first appearance since antiquity, both in theory and in practice, in the fifteenth century. It is expressed most vividly in Alberti's postulate that a church must be elevated on a high base and be clearly visible from all sides. What Alberti wishes to have understood as

Published as "Notizen zum kirchlichen Zentralbau der Renaissance" in *Studien zur toskanischen Kunst, Festschrift für L. H. Heydenreich* (Munich, 1964), pp. 157–165 a "monument" is the church building in its entirety. No doubt Christian churches always have had certain inherent monumental qualities, but Alberti gives to the concept a new and quite specific meaning. One is tempted to speak of an Albertian ideal of church beauty.[2]

This ideal could be realized only occasionally in the renovation and reconstruction of older cathedrals and parish or monastic churches; but with newly founded buildings it was attainable whenever they were erected on suitable sites. A site was suitable, however, only if it afforded an unobstructed view of the church and thereby allowed it to become a monument in Alberti's sense. Now, as it happens, the vast majority of centralized Renaissance churches were newly established buildings. It is certainly no accident that the three prime examples of the type, Santa Maria delle Carceri in Prato, Santa Maria della Consolazione in Todi, and Santa Maria presso San Biagio in Montepulciano, were all built *ex novo*. These churches have a number of fundamental elements in common:

1. They are visible from all sides.

2. From the earliest stage of construction on, their exteriors and interiors were given equal importance. The careful and rich incrustation of the exterior that distinguishes these buildings is by no means a matter of course in Italian Renaissance architecture.

3. The dome, too, is equally significant whether seen from within or without and cannot be interpreted from inside or outside alone. Inside it gives the effect of a high baldachin over the crossing; outside it crowns the monument.

4. The circle is used for the plan of the dome, even if it is not employed for the entire building.

5. The main altar holds a miraculous image.

6. Lastly, the histories of their founding are similar—an image of the Virgin begins to perform miracles, and the increasing number of devotees requires the erection of a church, which as a rule is soon replaced by a larger one.

When reading the histories of the founding of Marian churches, it is often hard to resist the thought that the attraction to the miraculous image—indeed, the very emergence of the image and its miracles—was due to the unconscious, or perhaps only unspoken, desire to erect a monument over it on a particular spot. Liturgical requirements for church services, for the establishment of new altars, or for the endowment of new Masses are scarcely ever mentioned. Rather, it is always the veneration of the miracle-working image itself that leads to the building of the church. Accordingly in the histories of these churches the architectural ideal—the esthetic ideal of the monument—is linked generally with strictly religious requirements and attitudes.

The entry in Luca Landucci's diary describing the undertaking of the construction of Santa Maria delle Carceri shows this combination of factors in the clearest way:

"At Prato in July of 1484 the populace began to worship an image of the Virgin Mary, which the whole city went to see. The image effected many miracles just as that of Bibbona [a village near Grosseto], causing the townspeople to initiate the construction [of a church] at a large expense."[3]

The churches of Prato, Todi, and Montepulciano were built by their communities, but a very similar combination of motives lay behind the founding of the papal church of Santa Maria della Pace in Rome. Around 1480 an image of the Virgin, which was in the little church of Sant'Andrea dei Aquarenariis, had been "severely damaged by a thrown stone and had thereupon begun to bleed. In view of Pope Sixtus IV's special devotion to the Mother of God, it is probable that this event caused the Supreme Pontiff to begin thinking of a new and worthy edifice. The miracle led to the subsequent renaming and redecorating of the church. Sant'Andrea became Santa Maria delle Virtù. Soon thereafter the Pope must have pledged to erect a new building in honor of Mary and the people, if God would bring to the land the peace for which it longed. When peace was concluded in the war with Milan and Naples on 12 December 1482, Sixtus marched in solemn procession to Santa Maria delle Virtù and renamed it Santa Maria della Pace. From 1482 until the death of the Pope, the church was granted special indulgences."[4]

Santa Maria della Pace belongs formally to the centralized type, even though the octagonal space beneath its dome is preceded by a short nave. From the beginning the building site in the center of the old city prevented an unobstructed view of the church, but four sides of the octagon were exposed and the building seems to have been set off from its surroundings originally far more than it is today.

The partly morphological, partly iconological elements described are also found in numerous churches dedicated to the Virgin that were erected in central and northern Italy during the later fifteenth and sixteenth centuries.[5] The centralized scheme was varied in these buildings according to local tradition or the origin of the architect, but they have in common their dedication to the Virgin, a great crowning dome (sometimes encircled by subsidiary ones), their erection *ex novo,* and their excellent locations on open sites, usually, though not always, outside of town.

A group of Carolingian churches has been collected under the title of Sancta Maria Rotunda, the form and dedication of which point clearly to the Pantheon, also known as Sancta Maria ad Martyres, as their prototype.[6] The Pantheon was still called Sancta Maria Rotunda in the Renaissance,[7] and it can be assumed that since it was both a Marian church and a monument of antiquity it was regarded in a general way as the *exemplum* for centrally-planned Marian churches of the early and high Renaissance. No matter how much they may differ from the Pantheon, these churches still share with it the same patron saint and centralized form.

No large-scale re-creation of the Pantheon was attempted during the Renaissance.[8] Insurmountable technical difficulties alone precluded any such attempt; the construction of a vault of so great a size with cemented masonry was unthinkable. But esthetic considerations probably also played a role: the shallow dome of the Pantheon, scarcely asserting itself in the cityscape, could not compare with the superelevated, crowning outer shell that was developed in the course of the fifteenth century. This state of affairs has been discussed in a description of Leonardo da Vinci's designs for the dome to be built over the crossing of the cathedral in Milan: "One of the most serious problems in the planning of any dome . . . lies in the difficulty of compensating for the discrepancy between the inner and outer vaulting. If one vaults . . . over the inscribed circle, a harmonious relationship can be attained in the interior, but one must then forgo the exterior effectiveness of the dome, which will be too small to assert itself against the mass of the building as a whole."[9]

Just how important the "exterior effectiveness of the dome" was for the architects of the early sixteenth century can be gauged from an unexecuted project by Antonio da Sangallo the Younger for the redesigning of the dome of Santa Maria della Pace in Rome, which had been built at the end of the fifteenth century (Figs. 34, 35). It has been pointed out that the project can be explained only if one assumes that Sangallo considered the existing dome "too ineffective from the outside. Thus he surmounted the low dome with a commanding false dome, selecting a steeper, higher profile."[10]

The only large building of the Renaissance that can be called a Sancta Maria Rotunda, Michele Sanmicheli's Santa Maria di Campagna near Verona, also illustrates the difficulties that prevented imitation of the Pantheon.[11] The dome of the church is double-shelled (Figs. 36, 37); the spherical, outer shell, which is made of wood, determines its external appearance. The inner shell, an eight-sided cloister vault, rises above an octagon inscribed within the cylinder of the outer walls. This construction made it possible for Sanmicheli to set the base of the heavy inner shell relatively low and that of the light outer shell relatively high, thereby giving both static and esthetic requirements their due. To be sure the discrepancy between interior and exterior remains unsatisfying. This could hardly be avoided, however, if a circular building—Sancta Maria Rotunda— was to be crowned by a dome that would be visible from a great distance.

Bramante's Tempietto of San Pietro in Montorio, erected over the spot where, according to legend, St. Peter was martyred, is the best known example of a second type of centralized building, one that can be called a memorial.[12] The origins of this type go back to the beginnings of Christianity. Early Christian memorials could be erected to honor a holy place as well as a reliquary, since a place in which a saint had stayed also was considered a reliquary.[13] There is clear evidence in Serlio for the interpretation of the Tempietto as a memorial: "It is not very large . . . and was constructed exclusively in commemoration of St. Peter because it is said that he was crucified on that site."[14]

Bramante gave his memorial a new form derived directly from the peripteros of antiquity. In contrast, therefore, to churches dedicated to the Virgin, its formal and iconographical prototypes are not identical. This may be the reason why the form of the Tempietto was never emulated.[15] The small, octagonal memorial of San Giovanni in Olio near San Giovanni a Porta Latina, built slightly later than the Tempietto in 1508 over the site of St. John the Evangelist's martyrdom, is related formally to it only in so far as it is a centrally-planned building. This is true as well of the Domine Quo Vadis memorial, "the round chapel on the Via Appia where Christ the Saviour appeared to Peter,"[16] which was erected for Cardinal Reginald Pole in the reign of Julius III (Fig. 38).

These three memorials share basic elements with churches of the Virgin in Prato, Todi, and Montepulciano:

1. The earlier and apparently modest sanctuaries that stood on the three spots were rebuilt and enlarged as monuments or memorials.[17]

2. The new churches are freely visible from all sides (and it is possible that this was also true of the earlier buildings).

3. Their exteriors were accentuated by sumptuous decoration (all the interiors have been altered by subsequent reconstruction or restoration).

The esthetic function of the dome in centralized buildings is revealed by Bramante's Tempietto. None of the ancient peripteroi offered a model for the insertion of a drum between the main body of the building and the hemisphere of the dome. The drum is a new element. The dome it carries—in contrast, for example, to the Temple of the Sibyl in Tivoli—is just as important for the exterior appearance as the ring of columns around the cella. The building owes more than a little of its effectiveness as a memorial to the crowning of its peristyle by the dome. On the other hand, the proportions of the interior, that is of the cella itself, remain unchanged with respect to its ancient models, its clear height measuring twice its width.[18]

Comparison of the two types of centralized building demonstrates that the most important element they share is their monumental character, the esthetic ideal codified by Alberti in his treatise. This conception of the sacral building attains its grandest expression in the projects for the rebuilding of St. Peter's. By destroying Constantine's basilica with its burden of tradition, Bramante gave the new memorial over the grave of the apostle a centralized form. It is no coincidence that Caradosso's medal, the only visual source that gives a reasonably clear picture of Bramante's project, shows the exterior of the building.

Important evidence for the emancipation of the centralized form is offered by Leonardo da Vinci's architectural studies. Only a few of these drawings can be connected with any specific building; the great majority probably were intended for Leonardo's projected architectural treatise, the didactic, pattern-book character of which has been pointed out.[19] The predominance of centralized structures in these studies reveals that for Leonardo the concept of a church was virtually synonymous with the concept of a centralized building. When, in another instance, Leonardo designs a circular mausoleum as a peripteral, domed building crowning a hilltop, a peripteros with a striking resemblance to Bramante's Tempietto,[20] he combines two characteristics also possessed by centralized religious buildings: it is at once a memorial and a monument in the more general sense that Alberti gives it.

Not every centralized building of the Renaissance falls readily into one of the two categories described. Since the early Cinquecento the pure, centralized form had been used for churches even when it had no iconographical significance. Santi Celso e Giuliano, for instance, was a collegiate church commissioned by Julius II;[21] and only artistic considerations can explain why Bramante chose a centralized form for the new building instead of the longitudinal plan one would have expected. This is also true of the confraternity church of Sant'Eligio degli Orefici, presumably designed by Raphael. These two buildings are testimony that in the course of the Cinquecento Alberti's ideal of the monument crowned by a dome became accepted independently of the iconographical tradition of the day, whereas in the Quattrocento it had still been tied to iconographical requirements.

Notes

1. See Rudolf Wittkower, *Architectural Principles,* pp. 4ff.

2. Alberti, *Architettura,* VII: 3.

3. *Diario Fiorentino dal 1450 al 1516,* J. del Badia, ed. (Florence, 1883), pp. 47ff.

4. G. Urban, "Die Kirchenbaukunst des Quattrocento in Rom," *Römisches Jahrbuch für Kunstgeschichte 9/10* (1961/62): pp. 176ff. (hereafter Urban, "Kirchenkunst").

5. See the examples cited in Wittkower, *Architectural Principles,* p. 18, #7-8.

6. See Richard Krautheimer, "Arte del Primo Millennio," *Atti del 11° Convegno per lo studio dell'arte dell'Alto Medio Evo, 1950,* Pavia, (Turin, 1953): pp. 21ff.

7. See, for example, the inscription "Pantheon idest S. Maria Rotunda" on the corresponding pages of the so-called Codex Coner (Ashby, "Drawings," Figs. 13, 35, 36). On the other hand, Serlio refers continuously to the "Pantheon" and only adds by way of explanation that "volgarmente se gli dice la Rotonda" because of its shape. Else-

where he mentions the consecration "al culto divino per Bonifatio Pontefice" (*Regole,* Introduction to III).

8. For classicistic "copies" of the Pantheon see C. L. V. Meeks, "Pantheon Paradigm," *Journal of the Society of Architectural Historians* 19 (1960): pp. 135ff (with mention as well of Palladio's Tempietto in Maser).

9. H. L. H. Heydenreich, *Die Sakralbaustudien Leonardo da Vincis* (Leipzig, 1929), p. 36; the "rewarding task of examining the technical development of this very interesting form" (*ibid.,* p. 37) has not yet, so far as I know, been undertaken. On the forms of domes in the Cinquecento see Giovannoni, *Saggi,* pp. 143ff.

10. Urban, "Kirchenkunst," p. 211.

11. The history of the building and a bibliography are found in the catalogue of the Sanmicheli Exhibition (Verona, 1960), pp. 181ff.

12. On the legends regarding the site of Peter's crucifixion see the literature in P. Pesci and E. Lavagnino,

S. *Pietro in Montorio*, Chiese di Roma Illustrate (1958), p. 5.

13. See A. Grabar, *Martyrium* (Paris, 1946), 1: pp. 29ff.

14. Serlio, *Regole*, III, 67v. The formal and religious significance of the Tempietto as a memorial was still very much alive in the seventeenth century, as the text of the Bollandists shows: ". . . rotundum sacellum, ductum (ut traditur) circum vestigium depactae olim Crucis, cujus vestigii memoriam semper recentem servaverint Christiani, quoad ipsum, Constantino imperante, fuit ejusmodi sacello ornatum" (*Acta Sanctorum, 29 June*). To my knowledge, the Constantinian founding of the Tempietto is not mentioned anywhere else.

15. S. Waetzoldt recently suggested that analogies to the Tempietto might be found in miniature religious architecture and, in this connection, referred to Fra Mariano da Firenze's description of the Tempietto— "Magnum marmoreumque ciborium columnis ornatum" ("Bemerkungen zu Bramantes Tempietto," *Sitzungsberichte der Kunstgeschichtlichen Gesellschaft zu Berlin* n.s. 11 [1962/63]: p. 13). The small aedicula on four columns with a statue of St. Andrew, which was erected for Pius II near the Ponte Milvio to commemorate the site on which he received the head of the saint in 1462, actually does have the form of a tabernacle or ciborium.

16. See G. B. Lugari, "Il sacello 'Domine, quo vadis' sulla Via

Appia," *Nuovo Bollettino di Archeologia Cristiana* 7 (1901): pp. 23ff.

17. In 1452 Nikolaus Muffel saw in San Pietro in Montorio "die Capell, do Sand Peter kreuzigt ist worden . . . sten noch die zwu seulen, dozwischen das creuz gestanden ist . . . und unter dem altar sol sein creutz begraben sein worden" (*Beschreibung der Stadt Rom*, W. Vogt, ed. [Tübingen, 1876], pp. 48ff). The words of the text seem to refer here, not to the old church of San Pietro in Montorio, but to a special structure on the site of the present Tempietto; the two columns of which Muffel speaks are also mentioned in a document of 1492. According to Fra Mariano da Firenze (see note 15), a "mons crucifixionis in medio claustri" was demolished when the Tempietto was built. Taken together, these sources point to the existence of an old memorial of some importance.

18. Compare Palladio's cross-section of the Temple of Sibyl in Tivoli with that of the Tempietto.

19. See L. H. Heydenreich, *Leonardo Architetto: seconda lettura Vinciana, 15 Aprile 1962* (Florence, 1963), p. 12.

20. See *ibid.*, p. 15 and Figs. 28–30.

21. According to Fra Mariano, ". . . titulusque cardinalis. Insuper collegium presbyterorum" (*Itinerarium Urbis Romae*, E. Bulletti, ed. [Rome, 1931], p. 69).

Postscript

See also S. Sinding Larsen, "Some Functional and Iconographical Aspects of the Centralized Church in the Italian Renaissance," in *Acta ad archaeologiam et artium historiam pertinentia*, 2 (1965): pp. 203ff.

3
SIXTEENTH-CENTURY ITALIAN SQUARES

The subject I will discuss may seem
to have little relevance to our modern world. The Italian squares of the
sixteenth century are situated in the center of old towns, far removed from
the main highways and the new suburbs that are the chief concern of
modern traffic experts and city planners. These squares were intended only
for pedestrians, or at the most for people on horseback, but certainly never
for the automobiles that today use them as parking lots. They were made
for individuals who lived and worked in their vicinity. The separation of
a man's place of work from his living quarters, so characteristic of today's
metropolis, was unknown before the early part of the nineteenth century.

Yet I am of the opinion that my subject is not concerned with the past
alone. When construction of a new subway system was recently undertaken
in Munich, the Mariensäule—the column of the Virgin that is the land-
mark of the city's main square—had to be removed, to be reinstalled later
at the same location. Similarily, the Hauptwache in Frankfurt, formerly
headquarters of the city constabulary, was dismantled and carefully set
aside in anticipation of its eventual re-erection. I might also remind you
of the strange fate of the Berlin Gedächtniskirche and its immediate surroundings, or of the restoration of the cathedral square at Freiburg im
Breisgau. In all these instances there is an almost instinctive desire to
preserve a link with the past in the very heart of the city, to retain a portion
of the original square even when, as in Berlin, all of the surrounding
buildings are completely rebuilt. Not only must practical considerations,
such as the rights of property owners, the buildings' functions, and traffic
demands, be taken into account; one also seeks to preserve the old and
combine it with the new, though frequently it would be easier and less
expensive to erect a totally new structure.

This phenomenon is very familiar to the historian of architecture. There

This paper was originally delivered as an address on the occasion of the nineteenth
annual meeting of the Max Planck Society, held in Mainz on 28 June 1968, and
published as "Italienische Plätze des 16. Jahrhunderts," in *Jahrbuch 1968 der
Max-Planck-Gesellschaft zur Förderung der Wissenschaften e. V.*, pp. 41–60

are but few instances of large buildings in which the architect was permitted to proceed in his design without regard to older structures; a building is rarely completed as originally planned by the architect. Architecture is distinguished from its sister arts, sculpture and painting, by the fact that its works undergo radical changes with time but nevertheless retain their artistic identity. The passage of time nearly always leaves its traces, not so much by actual decay as in the changes wrought in a building which is in continual use. It may be altered or rebuilt to serve a new purpose or to suit changing tastes. Time plays a very important part in any esthetic evaluation of a building. *Saxa loquuntur:* the same stones that reveal the creative genius of the architect are also eloquent witnesses to the passage of time, what men call history.

This interdependence of art and history can be deduced almost always from the architectural entity called a square.[1] In old cities the shape of the square, whether it was determined when the town was founded or resulted from the razing of existing structures, is no less subject to the alterations of time than are the surrounding buildings themselves. The Italian squares to be discussed are, for the most part, very old. They date back to antiquity and have remained in use ever since, but were given a new form in the sixteenth century.[2] Two examples may bring into focus the questions that challenge the architectural historian: the Piazza Erbe in Verona, which is surrounded by medieval buildings (Fig. 40), and the Piazza del Popolo in Fermo, which acquired its present shape in the sixteenth century (Fig. 41). In both cases the square occupies the site of the antique forum. The Roman forum of Verona undoubtedly had straight facades, and most probably was surrounded by the two-storied colonnaded buildings that were characteristic of the Greek agora and the Italic forum.

According to Vitruvius, the forum was used for mass meetings, gladiatorial contests, and as a marketplace; and money-changers had their shops within its loggias.[3] The Piazza Erbe serves as a market to this very day (Fig. 40). In Fermo only recently was the market moved from the piazza into a newly built market hall. Thus to some extent both squares fulfill the purpose for which they were created two thousand years ago. It is a fair assumption, although we have no absolute proof, that these squares remained in continuous use throughout the period of the migrations and the early Middle Ages. At what point, however, did the Piazza Erbe in Verona receive its present-day uneven alignment? Is this lack of uniformity typical of a square of the Middle Ages, and are the uniform and compact facades and loggias in Fermo peculiar to squares dating from the sixteenth century? Did the sixteenth century city fathers and architects of Fermo who erected the facades visible today know anything about the size and shape of their ancient forum? Was the square in Fermo planned as a unit or did it evolve in several building phases?

One of the most baffling of these problems is the continued existence throughout the Middle Ages of the one- or two-storied colonnaded buildings that surrounded the Roman forum (Fig. 39). In cases where the forum developed into a medieval square, the antique columns evidently disappeared at an early date and were replaced by a solid facade. With the single exception of the Piazza San Marco in Venice, which shall be discussed later, I know of no medieval square that is enclosed by colonnades. It is true that the medieval town halls normally had a loggia at ground level, where vendors sold their wares and justice was dispensed. The right to hold a market and judicial authority, two essential privileges of a township, found their concrete expression here; the community literally provided the protective roof over the local market. In some instances a loggia was erected next to the town hall for use by the city fathers on formal occasions. The best-known example of this is the Loggia dei Lanzi in Florence, which dates from the fourteenth century. One of the buildings that surround the Piazza Erbe in Verona (Fig. 40), the Casa dei Mercanti (merchants' guild hall), which was built in 1310, likewise has a loggia on the ground floor, intended for the display and sale of merchandise. Merchants met to discuss their business affairs in the hall above, in what today we might call the stock exchange. A comparison of the two squares clearly shows the insignificant contribution of the loggia of the Casa dei Mercanti in Verona, with its five bays, to the total appearance of the square; whereas in Fermo the image of the square as a unit became the subject of the architectural concept (Fig. 41), and the loggias give reality to this concept.

The image of a forum surrounded by arcades was handed down in antiquity by Vitruvius, and reappears in Italy around 1450 in the earliest important architectural treatise of the Renaissance, the *Ten Books on Architecture* of Leon Battista Alberti.[4] The many passages in this book taken almost word for word from Vitruvius leave no doubt that it was from him that Alberti borrowed his conception of a square. As far as can be determined, there was no square that conformed to Vitruvius's conception either in Alberti's native city of Florence or in any town with which he might have been familiar.

Shortly after 1460 another Florentine, the sculptor and architect
Filarete, who was strongly influenced by Alberti, described a square of
similar appearance. For Duke Francesco Sforza of Milan Filarete compiled
a manuscript describing a model town to be called Sforzinda. It was to
include two large squares, the Piazza dei Mercanti (Fig. 42), and the
"piazza dove si vende herbe et altri fructi," the marketplace proper where
perishable foodstuffs were sold (Fig. 43). Concerning the latter square he
writes: "In the first place, this square will be surrounded by porticoes
measuring ten *braccia* [about 5.6 meters] in width and supported by columns."[5] This description is followed by lists of the booths under the
arcades, in which fresh meat, fish, poultry, cheese, smoked meats, pastries,
vegetables, and fruit would be sold.

Filarete sets the dimensions of the marketplace at 200 by 100 *braccia*
(112 by 56 meters). The Piazza dei Mercanti, though somewhat smaller in
size—186 by 96 *braccia* (about 104 by 54 meters)—is nevertheless the
more important of the two. Its name, Merchants' Square, reflects the power
of the guilds. Around this piazza most of the town's public buildings were
to be erected. In the center the Palazzo Comunale was to be erected, with
its traditional open arcades at ground level.[6] The sides of the square are
provided with the customary loggias and include the Palazzo del Podestà,
the palace of the city's chief governing official; the chambers of the judges
and the offices of the notaries; the prison, custom house, and mint; a small
church; and finally, the shops of the jewelers and goldsmiths, the money-
changers' stalls, and the headquarters of the guilds.

Filarete's manuscript describes the residential city of a ruler, a model
city to be built without regard for any existing building. In short what he
had in mind was a utopia. Nevertheless, his manuscript throws light on
many of our current problems. In the first place, we can learn what sort
of buildings were customarily erected in a city's main square; this provides
a clear picture of the daily life in a piazza. Furthermore, the complete
separation of the food market from the Piazza dei Mercanti is of great
significance, a separation observed in the larger Italian cities to this day.
In Verona, for example, the public buildings such as the Palazzo Comunale
and the Palazzo del Podestà are not on the Piazza Erbe, the town market,
but at the neighboring square known today as the Piazza Dante.

In smaller cities the space available within the walls rarely allowed for
such a separation, so that one square usually had to suffice for both official
and commercial functions. This applies also to the Piazza Maggiore in

Vigevano, begun about 1490, which is the earliest extant example of a postantique square constructed at one time and surrounded by uniform loggias (Figs. 44–46). Vigevano was the birthplace and one of the seats of the Milanese Duke, Ludovico Sforza il Moro. An inscription still visible in the square explains the significance of the site.[7] In 1492, after some old houses adjoining the market had been torn down, Ludovico had the square widened and circumscribed by loggias, thereby improving its appearance. In 1492, work was begun on the square; two years later the paving was laid.[8] As the inscription reveals, it became virtually a new square in the process, its dimensions greatly exceeding those of the old marketplace. The facades are uniform on three sides: at the ground level relatively low loggias accommodated stores and workshops; above them rose two-storied dwellings. The facade of the newly erected Palazzo Comunale was integrated in this design, its only distinguishing mark being the municipal coat of arms, which has since disappeared.

The shops beneath the arcades correspond to Vitruvius's description of the Roman forum. The ground plan shows that the system of loggias continues across two streets that lead into the square, resulting in the preservation of the latter's unbroken outline.[9] Today the baroque facade of the cathedral takes up the fourth side of the square (Fig. 45). The fifteenth-century church was narrower and was flanked by a side street leading to the piazza. Construction of the present church was begun in 1532 and was completed only in the late seventeenth century. We know nothing about the facade of the old church; it may have been designed to conform to the unified image of the square. A contemporary source informs us that there was a daily small market and a weekly large one in the new square; however, the sale of fish and meat was banned. A slaughterhouse where meat was sold was provided at some distance from the town.

During the Middle Ages Vigevano achieved a certain distinction as the secondary seat of the Visconti, Dukes of Milan. Ludovico il Moro left very few of the medieval buildings standing. In their place he erected what was virtually a new town, of which the most famous landmarks are the piazza and the giant Castello Sforzesco. There is evidence that Bramante, then architect to the Duke of Milan, was involved in the construction of the castle at Vigevano. Later Bramante designed and began the rebuilding of St. Peter's in Rome for Pope Julius II, an undertaking that, because of its vast dimensions, was considered wildly utopian by his contemporaries; in fact, it took over one hundred years to complete.

In Rome, Bramante earned the title *Il Ruinante*,[10] the wrecker, because of his destruction of the old basilica of St. Peter's, which dated from the time of Constantine the Great. According to one contemporary source, he may have earned this nickname as the result of his earlier activities in Vigevano.[11] Although this report does not specifically mention the square, such a sobriquet can only derive from his destruction of the old marketplace and the medieval buildings. The demolition of these buildings and the creation of the new square in Vigevano are undoubtedly also an expression of Ludovico's own zeal for building. However, this does not account for the piazza's artistic significance. The year 1485 marked the appearance of the first printed edition of Alberti's *Ten Books on Architecture,* in which the designing of a square and its arcades is discussed at length. Alberti, borrowing almost word for word from Vitruvius, describes the Greek agora as being surrounded by two-storied loggias.[12] It is no coincidence that the Sforza inscription of Vigevano echoes Alberti's text so closely.[13] There is no absolute proof that Bramante was familiar with Alberti's treatise, but he was active at the Sforza court in the same years that Leonardo da Vinci was, and Leonardo did own a copy of the 1485 edition of Alberti's book.[14] Also, there are frequent references to Alberti in Leonardo's writings. It is quite unlikely that the two artists never discussed the book, published shortly before the alterations of the square in Vigevano—the more so since Leonardo worked as an architect in Milan.

Immense proportions; generous, and at the same time ruthless, planning, different from that of all of his contemporaries; the free use of the antique without slavish imitation: these are the hallmarks of Bramante's Roman works, and they are found as well in the piazza at Vigevano. A comparison of it with the square of Pienza in southern Tuscany, constructed thirty years earlier (Figs. 48, 49), reveals the extent to which the layout of Vigevano departs from the traditional and even from what, at the end of the fifteenth century, was considered modern. Pienza is also a princely creation. Pope Pius II Piccolomini, upon his elevation to the papacy, commissioned the architect Bernardo Rossellino to plan a new city to be called Pienza in his honor. In the main square were erected the cathedral of the newly formed bishopric, the town hall, and the palaces of the bishop and the Piccolomini family.[15] As in Vigevano, the magnificent buildings honored the birthplace of a ruler; the Palazzo Piccolomini corresponds in its functions to the Castello of Vigevano. The extent of the Piazza at Pienza, which is nearly square, is confined in one direction by the edge of the hillside on which the town is set. Yet, since the buildings were all new, it would have been possible to have expanded the square freely in the opposite direction, and above all to have surrounded it with loggias. Nevertheless, Rossellino followed the medieval pattern for a city square: only the town hall received a loggia at ground level, while the remaining buildings were given unbroken facades.

The squares of Pienza and Vigevano differ not only in dimensions but more significantly in character. The type of antique forum described by Vitruvius and later by Alberti appears first in Vigevano around 1490. The shape of the square corresponds exactly to the literary sources, which, although only implicitly cited in the Sforza inscription, were readily understood by the fifteenth-century humanist. According to Vitruvius and Alberti, the loggias of the antique forum were two-storied. The upper arcades afforded a view of the activities taking place in the square below. The loggias of Vigevano are single-storied and the space above them is used for dwellings. This departure from the ancient precept is most easily explained by the fact that the Duke probably was more interested in a steady income from his tenants than in spectator fees from the occasional tournaments held in the square. At any rate, the square's facades were given a uniform ornamental design, so that the three original sides appear as an unbroken front, rather than as rows of individual buildings.

A decade after Vigevano, the main square in Ascoli Piceno was rebuilt (Figs. 47, 50, 51). Ascoli, located near Ancona on the Adriatic coast, was a free city during the Middle Ages but was incorporated into the Papal States in 1506. Shortly thereafter, between 1507 and 1509, the three sides of the rectangular Piazza del Popolo, which incidentally occupies the site of an ancient forum, were given uniform, two-storied fronts that conceal the irregularly shaped medieval houses.[16] The only buildings left unaltered were the Franciscan church on one of the short sides of the square, and the Palazzo Comunale on the long side. Although both of these older structures are much taller than the new loggias with their additional stories, the square as a whole represents a carefully balanced composition. The majestic facade of the Palazzo Comunale is flanked by the new colonnades on both sides; on the longer, opposite side the colonnades are continuous, and the small street leading into the square is scarcely noticeable (Figs. 50, 51). The transept and dome of the church are counterweights to the Palazzo Comunale; and the campanile emphasizes one corner of the square (Fig. 50). At the other corner is the church portal, which is adorned with a monument to Julius II, who incorporated Ascoli into the Papal States. Significantly, the arcades adjoining the portal are not in exact alignment with the Palazzo Comunale (Fig. 47). Owing to a slight bend in the alignment, the papal monument can be seen clearly from the square; otherwise, it would have been partly obscured by the loggias. Both the colonnades and the monument were put up simultaneously and are in unmistakable relationship to each other.

Strangely enough, there is no clue as to the identity of the artist who designed the colonnades and the monument. The former were largely completed by 1509, and in 1510 the latter was dedicated. A relatively obscure Lombard named Bernardino da Carona is known to have been active in Ascoli as a stonemason and builder between 1504 and 1510, but it is not likely that he could have been responsible for such an unusual design.[17] More probably, the remodeling was undertaken at the behest of the papal legate, since it occurred immediately following the annexation of Ascoli by the Pope, whose monument is a prominent feature of the new square. It is conceivable that a Roman architect was responsible for the new design.

Since there is a close relationship between the squares of Vigevano and Ascoli Piceno, it can be assumed that the architect who rebuilt the square in Ascoli was familiar with Vigevano. Admittedly, though, there is a basic difference between the two projects. The Sforza Duke destroyed the medieval city in order to construct his gigantic square. In Ascoli the older square was considerably reduced in size by the new colonnades and two important buildings of the old square were retained. The careful preservation of the old features is no less impressive than are the uniformity and harmony of the square's new appearance. Moreover, in Ascoli the stories above the loggias carry a terrace from which, as in the Roman forum, it is possible to survey the activities taking place in the square below (Fig. 50). It can only be assumed that here again Alberti's treatise was the guiding influence.

The colonnades of Vigevano and Ascoli still serve as shops, and a market is also held regularly in both squares. But our next example, the Piazza Santissima Annunziata in Florence, which reminds one of Vigevano and Ascoli in more than one respect, has never been used as a marketplace (Figs. 52, 53). This square was not created in a single building campaign. When the Church of the Santissima Annunziata was erected in the thirteenth century, the monks also acquired the area in front of the church.

The oldest of the buildings that surround the square today is the Loggia degli Innocenti, the loggia of the Foundlings' Home, designed by Brunelleschi in the early part of the fifteenth century. Around 1450 a one-bay porch was built in front of the high wall that closed off the square from the atrium lying directly in front of the church. In 1516 the monks began to build a loggia on the long side opposite the Foundlings' Home, copying Brunelleschi's colonnades of one hundred years earlier.[18] It was only with the building of the second loggia that the area, which until then had been enclosed by various types of buildings, became a true piazza. Around 1600 the single-bay loggia in front of the atrium was enlarged right and left to form a colonnade of seven bays. As a result, the square was now surrounded by colonnades on three sides.

In this connection special attention should be paid to the copy of Brunelleschi's loggia in the square. The replica was designed by Antonio da Sangallo the Elder and Baccio d'Agnolo; the loggia was completed in 1525 and the residences above it in 1540. The building was commissioned and paid for by the monks. The living quarters were not intended for the monks' use, but were to be rented out to increase the monastery's revenue. It may be concluded that the loggia always had an esthetic rather than a practical function. This is the only way to explain the phenomenon, rare for the sixteenth century, of an exact copy having been made of a building that was erected a century earlier. The loggia was constructed in order to create a piazza bordered by colonnades. The piazza, viewed as an entity, thus becomes the realization of an artistic concept. Here also a square that was not used as a marketplace could retain the shape of a Roman forum, surrounded by loggias.

This also explains the high podium on which the new loggia stands and the absence of shops beneath its arcades. Since the square did not serve as a marketplace, shops could be dispensed with. The podium is modeled on that of the Foundlings' Home, where, as in many Tuscan hospitals, it had the function of separating the hospital area from the square and its traffic. The podium of the 1516 loggia served no such purpose; it owes its existence to the desire to provide uniform facades for both sides of the square.

In 1516, Baccio d'Agnolo, one of the architects of the loggia, was paid for a model of the facade of the Church of San Lorenzo in Florence, which had been designed by Jacopo Sansovino. The latter certainly knew of the plans for the new loggia in the Piazza Santissima Annunziata. And this detail is not without significance, for two decades later Sansovino altered the Piazza San Marco in Venice (Figs. 54–59).[19]

By and large, the main square in Venice appears to have reached its present dimensions as early as the late twelfth century; a late thirteenth century chronicle tells us that by that time it was enclosed by loggias. It is also worth noting that we are dealing here with the only fully documented medieval example of the type in Italy. A painting by Gentile Bellini, dated 1496, shows the old Piazza San Marco visited by a religious procession (Fig. 56). It is a matter of record that from the late thirteenth century tournaments, equestrian events, and other festivities were held there; and one is reminded of Vitruvius' account of the performances that took place in the ancient fora. The Venetians probably adopted the ancient shape of the square from the East, possibly from Byzantium. Their city, built on the lagoon in the Middle Ages, owes its magical fairy-tale quality to the fact that antiquity, brought back to Italy from the Greek East, was here preserved through the alterations that were made.

It is true that the Piazza San Marco has changed since the thirteenth century. Bellini depicts, on the left of his *Procession in the Piazza San Marco,* the fifteenth-century loggia of the Procurazie Vecchie and, on the right, the hospice of San Marco, a thirteenth-century building, the facade of which is aligned with the campanile of San Marco. This hospice was torn down in the sixteenth century to make room for the Procurazie Nuove. The facade of the new building was not constructed on the foundations of the demolished hospice but was set back, so that the square became wider than it had been previously. The distance between the old and the new facade is 24 meters at the campanile and 13 meters at the other corner of the square. As a result, the square grew from 60 to 80 meters on the east side and from 45 to 55 meters on the west side (Fig. 54).

The square owes its altered shape to Jacopo Sansovino, who began to build the new library of San Marco at the corner nearest the campanile in 1537. In so doing he placed the corner of the building at a distance of about 5 meters from the campanile. The library's three bays, which face the campanile, also determined the front of the adjacent Procurazie Nuove, erected somewhat later. A book written about Venice, published by Sansovino's son Francesco in 1561 during his father's lifetime, confirms that it was Jacopo Sansovino and not the architect of the Procurazie Nuove who first decided on this alignment: "The large library building shall extend to the side of San Geminiano [the church then situated across the square from San Marco and later torn down (Fig. 85)] and from here shall continue around the square as far as the clock tower."[20]

Although the project of rebuilding the Procurazie Vecchie was never carried out, Sansovino did decisively alter the old square: the church of San Marco now occupies the middle of the square's east side, whereas formerly its right flank was approximately in line with the south side; the campanile, which stood originally in the corner between the Piazza and the Piazzetta and which was joined on both sides to the old facade but not quite aligned with it, became now a freestanding monument, with the library's two facades forming a right angle at the corner. Furthermore, the southwest corner of the Piazza, originally an acute angle, now appears to form a true right angle, although in reality the angle measures slightly more than 90 degrees.

Scarcely less significant was Sansovino's transformation of the Piazzetta, which extends at a right angle from the Piazza and is flanked by the Doges' Palace and the library. Here Sansovino's new building replaced an old and rather nondescript structure, as earlier city views show. As far as can be determined, this "panatteria" had no loggias. Sansovino's library has two stories: the upper one houses the reading rooms and book stacks, and the lower one is designed as a loggia. But it could do without a loggia; from the very beginning the shops connected with it were either rented out or were used by the procurators as offices.

Sansovino adopted the arcade motif of the old piazza facades on the short side of the library facing the piazza. On the other hand, the loggias of the long side on the Piazzetta were an innovation, conceived to create a unified entity by consolidating the Piazza and the Piazzetta. The library's majestic front on the Piazzetta acts as a counterweight to the facade of the Doges' Palace opposite; the delicate proportions of the two-storied Gothic arcade balance the cornices and the half-columns copied from antiquity.[21] In so doing, Sansovino succeeded in creating a square formed by walls disparate in form yet which together present an unforgettably harmonious appearance.

Sansovino's library was begun in 1537. The following year Pope Paul III ordered the equestrian statue of Marcus Aurelius, which then was installed outside the basilica of San Giovanni in Laterano in Rome, to be set up at the Capitol. This was the first step toward the modernization of the only Italian square that in importance and beauty can rival the Piazza San Marco. Many questions concerning the creation and interpretation of Michelangelo's Piazza del Campidoglio still remain unanswered. I shall limit myself to just a few observations (Figs. 60–63).[22] It is not known when Michelangelo made his definitive design for the square, nor are there any autograph drawings for it. The most important sources for it are two engravings by the French artist Étienne Dupérac, made in 1568 and 1569, which, according to their captions, represent Michelangelo's plan (Fig. 61); Michelangelo himself had died in 1564.

By and large, Dupérac's representations correspond to the present appearance of the square. It is true, of course, that the buildings were erected at different times; in some instances, long after Michelangelo's death and the publication of the engravings. The facade of the Palazzo Senatorio, the rear of which faces the Forum Romanum, conceals an older structure, which since the Middle Ages had been the residence of the senator who was the city's nominal leader. The double flight of steps in front of the facade dates from between 1544 and 1553. In 1561, work was begun on the Palazzo dei Conservatori, the building housing the executive branch of the city government and situated on the west flank of the square. While this involved only the remodeling of an older structure, the so-called Palazzo Nuovo on the opposite, east side of the square was built *ex novo* in the seventeenth century. Literary sources confirm that in the last three years of his life Michelangelo occupied himself with designs for the facade of the Palazzo dei Conservatori; and he was also responsible for the building activity then underway on the Palazzo Senatorio.

Even though the written and visual evidence relating to Michelangelo's project for the Capitol leaves a great deal unexplained, there is no compelling reason to doubt the correctness of Dupérac's captions, which state that his engravings represent Michelangelo's design. Several views of the square, made before and during the reconstruction, give additional information regarding the shape and condition of the area that Michelangelo set out to redesign (Fig. 60). The piazza was unpaved; the fifteenth century Palazzo dei Conservatori had a loggia on the ground floor; the fortresslike Palazzo Senatorio had three stories of equal height and a tower rising to one side of the middle axis; and at the top of the hill was the long flank of the medieval church of Santa Maria in Aracoeli.

Michelangelo provided new facades for both of the old palaces; he reduced the width of the square by means of an entirely new building, which is a counterpart to the Palazzo dei Conservatori; and he designed the unique pattern of the pavement and erected the equestrian monument of Marcus Aurelius on its present location. A double flight of steps was built in front of the Palazzo Senatorio, and the tower now appears in the structure's middle axis. A ramp, bordered on either side by a balustrade and leading from the city street up to the square, further accentuates the middle axis.

Michelangelo's Capitoline square has many features that are common to all the other squares discussed so far: heterogeneous older buildings are allowed to become part of a homogeneous whole; the space now reveals fully the artist's intention; and no architectural element in the ensemble is left to chance. At the Capitol, it is as though one were in a room with clearly defined spatial limits; within this room the equestrian statue provides the central focal point. In this connection it is scarcely necessary to mention that two of the three buildings around the Capitoline square have loggias at the ground level. Michelangelo, in his characteristic way, here repeats what had been done a generation earlier in the Piazza Santissima Annunziata. The Roman guilds had their official quarters on the ground floor of the Palazzo dei Conservatori; the loggias thus had a definite function as anterooms and entrances to these offices. On the other hand, the Palazzo Nuovo, built much later, served no practical purpose as such. Like the Florentine loggia of 1516, its sole function was to complete the square with uniform facades on the two long sides. Michelangelo had been in Florence in 1516 and there could have observed the erection of the copy of the famous Loggia degli Innocenti.

The facades of Michelangelo's twin palaces are at acute angles to the Palazzo Senatorio but at an obtuse angle to the balustrade. Michelangelo did not alter the sharp angle between the two existing buildings when he remodeled them. The alignment of the Palazzo Nuovo, including the angle which it forms with the Palazzo Senatorio, corresponds exactly to its prototype across the way, as does the facade itself. The trapezoid of the ground plan of the square results from the decision to erect twin buildings. It is most revealing that at first glance one imagines the square to be rectangular rather than trapezoidal. This is not so much an optical illusion as the result of artistic calculation.

As the engravings show, Michelangelo intended to surround the patterned pavement of the square with three concentric oval steps. The combination of trapezoid and oval has the effect of making the viewer think that the four angles of the trapezoid are identical; instinctively one assumes it to be a rectangle. By the same token, since the larger axis of the oval is at right angles to the Palazzo Senatorio and to the balustrade, one is made to believe that the shorter axis also bisects the facades of the twin buildings at a right angle. Consequently, the two facades give the illusion of being parallel.

The peculiar curves of the pavement's ornamentation radiate outward from the statue in the center and lead the eye back to it. The statue seems to be mounted on a double base: the oval socle on which it stands and a larger oval, which occupies the central area of the square. This larger base establishes the architectural relationship of the statue to the square; the statue thereby acquires monumental proportions. As a result, the Roman emperor's equestrian monument, the work of a sculptor, becomes the gravitational center of an architectural composition which is created by another sculptor, one who received Roman citizenship in this square in 1536.

The Piazza del Campidoglio has been compared frequently with the square in Pienza, which has a similar trapezoidal ground plan, and the question has been raised of the relationship between Michelangelo's design and that of the square of Pius II, completed nearly a century earlier. The square in Pienza is situated on the ridge of a hill that runs at a right angle to its main axis. The pavement design is intended to be viewed by a spectator who approaches the square from the somewhat lower marketplace and who enters it from the side of the Palazzo Comunale. From this vantage point, the facades of the cathedral and of the buildings on either side present a stage backdrop. The diverging walls of the side buildings and the striped pavement pattern result in a perspective in reverse, and the distance between the cathedral facade and the viewer is diminished by the perspective. On the other hand, the pavement pattern reveals the true dimensions. Both devices work together to intensify the effect created by the principal facade. Moved closer to the spectator by means of an optical trick, it appears higher and wider than it actually is.[23] Despite the similarity in form between the two squares, the divergence of the Capitoline facades has an effect very different from that created in Pienza. Michelangelo wished neither to intensify the perspective of the Palazzo Senatorio nor to create one ideal vantage point from which it is to be viewed. The ground plan of his design is perceived more as a rectangle than as a trapezoid. The piazza in Pienza, on the other hand, contains no element that might induce the viewer to disregard its true shape.

The comparison with Pienza reveals how much more Michelangelo's Capitoline square gives the effect of a closed area in whose confines the visitor is expected to move and circumambulate the equestrian statue. He is not expected, as in Pienza, to take in the entire space at one glance from any specific spot. Although the striped pattern of Pienza's pavement is not compatible with his conception of the Piazza del Campidoglio, Michelangelo evidently wanted to employ such a design for another Roman square. In 1548 he completed the facade of the Palazzo Farnese; a year later an engraving representing the new facade appeared (Figs. 64, 65).[24] It shows a checkerboard pattern on the square in front of the facade. In the preceding years the Farnese family had bought up the houses that used to occupy what is now the square and had them torn down. Thus the laying out of the square coincided with the building of their palace, and the engraving may well represent Michelangelo's proposal for paving the square. The geometrical pattern, which was never carried out, would have given the square a scale that could have been easily understood. The square blocks of pavement and the bays of the palace facade are identical in width; in other words, the width of the facade and its components would have been projected on the pavement. A viewer standing across the square from the palace would have been able to estimate its width by referring to the paving stones lying directly at his feet. Here, too, as in the Piazza del Campidoglio, the pavement was assigned a significant role in the architectural composition.

It is clear that Michelangelo's design for the Piazza del Campidoglio and Sansovino's replanning of the Piazza San Marco were widely known long before their final execution and were already causing repercussions in the sixteenth century, although no other square can equal them in artistic invention and significance. Yet mention should be made of one last square that was redesigned at about the same time as the Piazza del Campidoglio: the Piazza Maggiore in Bologna, the second city of the Papal States (Figs. 66–68). The medieval Church of San Petronio and the Palazzo del Podestà,[25] the municipal courthouse, rebuilt in the fifteenth century, occupy the long sides. In 1555, the Palazzo Comunale, situated on the short, west side, received a monumental portal, the position of which was determined by the square's middle axis (Fig. 66). Around 1560 a uniform facade, known as the Portico dei Banchi, was erected on the short, east side of the square to cover up numerous unsightly medieval houses the loggias of which were used for stores and workshops (Fig. 67). The Italian word *banco* originally meant shop counter or trestle, and by extension it came to mean a money-changer's stall or bank. The Portico dei Banchi refers to the money-changers' stalls which, according to Vitruvius, were placed within the porticoes of the Roman forum. Today, whenever a foreigner changes his money into *lire* at one of the banks at the Portico dei Banchi in Bologna, he uses the same type of building as the one in which Greeks and Egyptians exchanged their *sesterces* for *denarii* two thousand years ago in the Roman forum.

The design for the Portico dei Banchi made by Giacomo Barozzi da Vignola has been preserved (Fig. 69);[26] actually, it was realized in a somewhat simpler version. The two streets leading into the square on the side of the Portico dei Banchi are bridged by arches so that, as in Vigevano, the street exits are subordinated to the plan of the piazza. The top cornice of the portico is placed at about the same height as that of the older Palazzo del Podestà and the Palazzo Comunale. Here too the sixteenth century alterations, with their unification of uneven facades and their regulation of width and height, have created a square of harmonious proportions. Unfortunately the little clock towers that Vignola had planned to be built over the two arches to accentuate the facade were never built.

With the exception of Pienza and Vigevano, all of the examples discussed deal with the remodeling of older squares whereby their existing facades were given a more uniform look and were made part of a new entity. Nowhere does one encounter a rigid symmetry on all four sides; the goal has been to substitute order for the previous disorder. The viewer is asked to experience the square as a man-controlled space and as an area surrounded by similar, yet not necessarily identical, facades. To achieve this, older squares were doubled in size, buildings that served no useful purpose were included in the plan, while venerable old structures, such as the Hospice of San Marco, were demolished; even one of the Capitol's fabled landmarks, the Church of Santa Maria in Aracoeli, vanished behind a new building.

The striving for order and uniformity also finds its expression in the architectural theories of the sixteenth century. The theoreticians were obviously familiar with Vitruvius's treatise, written at the time of Emperor Augustus, and with Alberti's textbook. In the Renaissance, theory usually developed out of practical considerations. The colonnades of the square at Vigevano are illustrative of one of the rare instances in which the reverse is true.

The squares discussed were conceived between 1460 and 1570; yet the designing of squares was also one of the great themes of Italian architecture in the Middle Ages and in the Baroque. The Renaissance examples, however, are strikingly different, both in composition and orchestration, from the squares of earlier and later periods. The square at Todi, for instance, is one of the most beautiful medieval examples, but it has buildings that vary considerably in height and width and has a nearly rectangular ground plan (Fig. 70). The majestic Palazzo Comunale, with its flight of steps, dominates the scene. On the other hand, in the Renaissance square one observes the conscious attempt to create uniformity and to make the new harmonize with the old. In addition to their harmonious facades, all sixteenth-century squares have in common the fact that their loggias were designed to human proportions. Whether one strolls amid the colonnades or walks into the square, one is always able to relate one's height to that of the columns and piers of the arcades; hence the security and intimacy so characteristic of these squares. The height of their facades is measurable, not immense as in the Piazza of St. Peter's.

The architects and city fathers who constructed these squares rarely found it necessary to destroy existing buildings; they preferred to reconcile the new with the old, to preserve whatever could be preserved. In so doing, they did not bind themselves to any rigid scheme. The urge to create new forms was always tempered by respect for what already existed. Reverence for the historic past explains why old Italian squares are hardly ever alike.

Standing in the square at Todi, time seems to have stopped since the late Middle Ages. Moving about in the squares of Venice, Bologna, and Rome, however, one feels that, figuratively speaking, they have continued to grow. They provide the setting for past history as well as for the living present. If a sense of history is one of the special attributes of man, then here in these squares, more than anywhere else, the realization is granted to him of how much the past conditions his present and future existence. This paradox has been beautifully expressed by T. S. Eliot:

> Time present and time past
> Are both perhaps present in time future
> And time future contained in time past.[27]

Notes

1. A bibliography on the subject is found in P. Lavedan, *Histoire de l'Urbanisme*, 2d. ed., 3 vols. (Paris, 1959).

2. See Giovannoni, *Saggi*, pp. 267–306.

3. Vitruvius, *De architectura* V:1, M. H. Morgan, trans. (1914).

4. Alberti, *Architettura* p. 714.

5. Filarete, *Treatise*, II: Book 10, fol. 73 *verso* and 71 *recto*.

6. *Ibid.*—". . . e detto [palace] è tutto pilastri quadri di sotto e tutto in volta da quali sono rette da questi pilastri."

7. It also mentions the draining of the marshes in the vicinity of the city: See Latin inscription with translation in Chapter 4, Note #13 and text.

8. See Colombo, "Piazza Ducale," pp. 248ff.

9. Alberti had already recommended that the streets leading into the square be vaulted over. *De re ædificatoria* (1966), p. 717.

10. See L. Pastor, *Popes* 6: p. 478.

11. Unpublished communication of Professor J. S. Ackerman. Bramante was also responsible for supervising building supplies used in Vigevano; see L. Beltrami, *Bramante a Milano, Nuovi Documenti* (Milan, 1912), p. 12.

12. "Forum græci quadratum constituebant porticibus amplissimis et duplicibus circuibant" (*De re ædificatoria*, p. 715).

13. " . . . circa Forum aream ampliavit ac porticibus circumductis in hanc speciem exornavit"; see Chapter 4, note #13.

14. A manuscript of Leonardo, recently discovered in Madrid, includes a list of books owned by him shortly after 1500, among which is *Batista Alberti in architettura;* see L. Reti, "The Two Unpublished Manuscripts of Leonardo da Vinci in the Biblioteca Nacional of Madrid," II, *The Burlington Magazine* 110 (1968): p. 81.

15. See L. H. Heydenreich, "Pius II als Bauherr von Pienza," *Zeitschrift für Kunstgeschichte* 6 (1937): pp. 105ff. (hereafter, Heydenreich, "Pius II"); and E. Carli, *Pienza—La Città di Pio II* (Siena, 1966), p. 46 (hereafter Carli, *Pienza*).

16. See G. Fabiani, *Ascoli nel Cinquecento* (Ascoli Piceno, 1959), 2: p. 202.

17. According to a document dated 1509, the design of the workshops and the stores beneath the arcades was carried out ". . . secundum forman capitulorum veterum factorum aliis fabricatoribus plateæ et secundum designum factum per ipsos" (G. Fabiaini, *Cola dell'Amatrice secondo i Documenti* [Ascoli Piceno, 1952], p. 194). The design referred to here, the originator of which is not named in the document, might have been the work of the architect in charge. Bernardino da Carona executed the monument to Julius II on the square; however, it is not known from the documents whether the payments he received covered the actual execution of the work only or the design as well; see *ibid.*, p. 199. The same is also true of his involvement in the construction of the Loggia dei Nobili, adjacent to the Piazza del Popolo; see G. Castellani, "La Chiesa di S. Michele in Fano e gli

artisti che vi lavorarono," *Studia Picena* 3 (1927): pp. 163, 180.

18. See J. del Badia, "La Loggia a destra nella Piazza della SS. Annunziata di Firenze," *Arte e Storia* 1 (1882): pp. 82ff. Concerning the church and its atrium, see W. and E. Paatz, *Kirchen* 1: pp. 604ff.

19. See W. Lotz, "Sansovinos Bibliothek von S. Marco und die Stadtbaukunst der Renaissance," *Kunst des Mittelalters in Sachsen: Festschrift für Wolf Schubert* (Weimar, 1967), pp. 336ff. (hereafter Lotz, "Sansovinos Bibliothek").

20. Cf. *Delle Cose Notabili che sono in Venezia*, Venice, 1561, p. 22. In the foreword Francesco Sansovino, whose name does not appear on the title page, writes that he is the author of the book. A similar remark on the planning of the piazza, found in Francesco Sansovino's *Venezia Città Nobilissima*, Venice, 1581, fol. 112, is quoted in G. Lorenzetti, "La Libreria Sansoviniana di Venezia," *Accademie e Biblioteche d'Italia*, 2 (1928–29): p. 87.

21. See Chapter 5.

22. Concerning the redesigning of the Capitol in the sixteenth century, see Ackerman, *Michelangelo* 1: pp. 54ff.; 2: pp. 49ff.; and G. de Angelis d'Ossat et al., *Il Campidoglio di Michelangelo* (Milan, 1965), passim.

23. See Heydenreich, "Pius II," passim.

24. See Ackerman, *Michelangelo* 1: p. 88, #20.

25. See F. Malaguzzi Valeri, *L'Architettura a Bologna nel Rinascimento* (Bologna, 1899), pp. 109ff.

26. Berlin, Kupferstich-Kabinett, Staadliche Museen; see M. Walcher Casotti, *Il Vignola* (2 vols., Trieste, 1960) 1: pp. 62ff., 147ff; and W. Lotz, "Vignola-Zeichnungen," *Jahrbuch der Preussischen Kunstsammlungen* 59 (1938): p. 105.

27. *Four Quartets*, lines 1–3.

Postscript

Since this study was published in 1968, the literature on the urban environment, on urbanization in general and, consequently, on piazze has multiplied enormously. A satisfactory, though far from complete, bibliography may be found in Franco Borsi and Geno Pampaloni, *Le Piazze* (Monumenti d'Italia vol. 1), (Novara, 1975), pp. 489ff. For the Piazza San Marco, see my postscript to Chapter 5.

34. Antonio da Sangallo the Younger, project for the dome of Santa Maria della Pace, Rome; Florence, Uffizi A 702 (photo: Florence, Gab. Fot. Naz.)

35. Rome, Santa Maria della Pace, octagon and stepped dome (photo: Bibliotheca Hertziana)

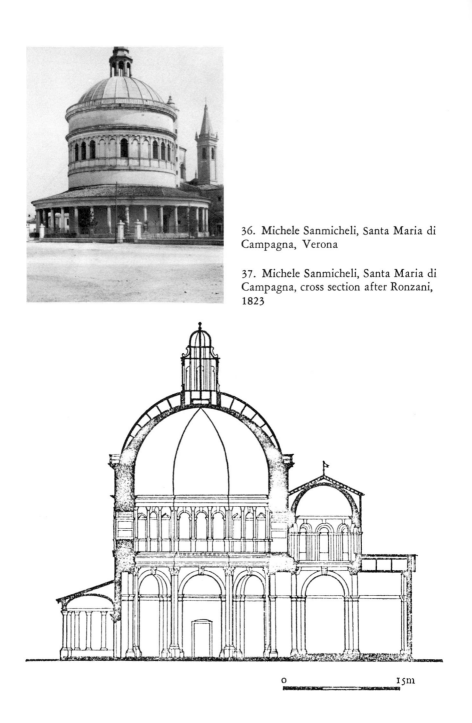

36. Michele Sanmicheli, Santa Maria di Campagna, Verona

37. Michele Sanmicheli, Santa Maria di Campagna, cross section after Ronzani, 1823

0   15m

38. Rome, Domine Quo Vadis; from *Acta Sanctorum,* 28 (Luglio), 7: 395

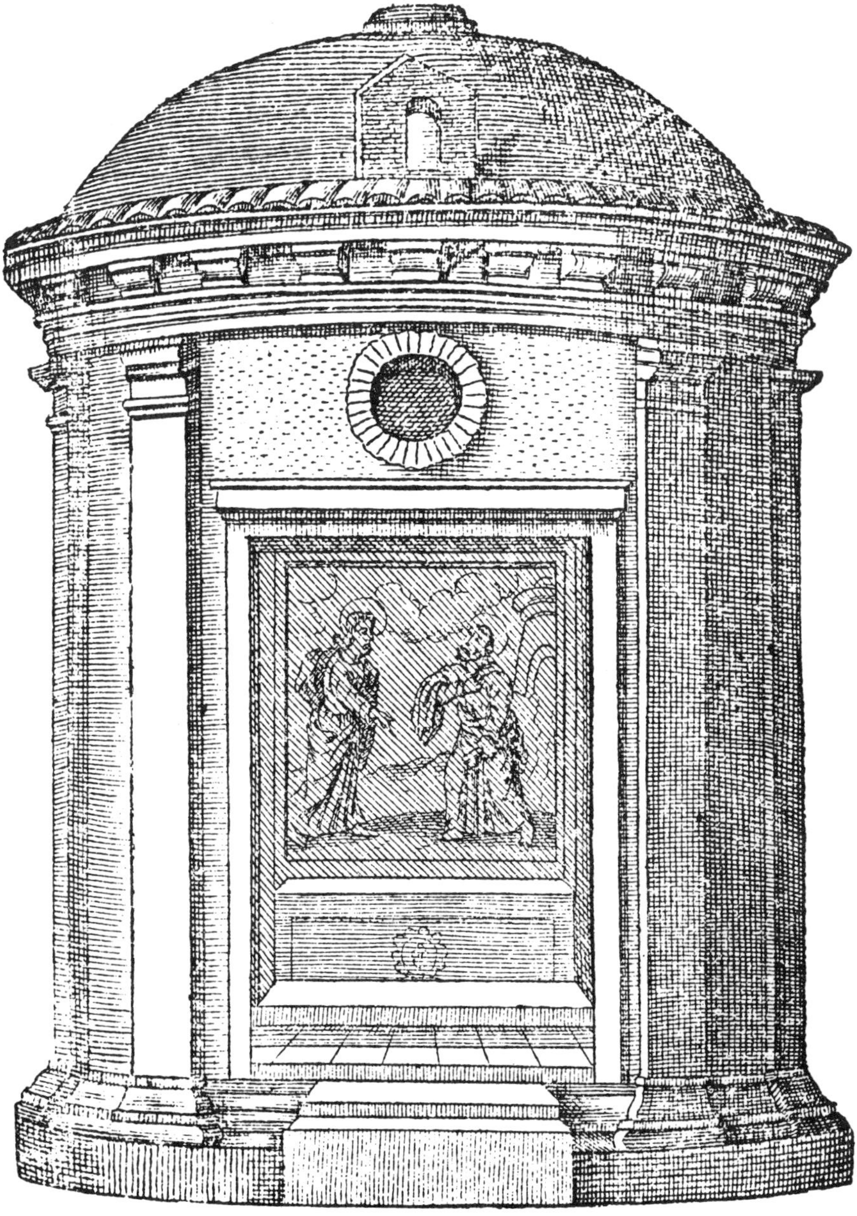

40. Verona, Piazza Erbe (photo: Verona, Vera)

39. Pompeii, ruins of the loggias at the Forum (photo: Rome, Deutsches Archäologisches Institut)

41. Fermo, Piazza del Popolo (photo:
Fermo, Moscoloni)

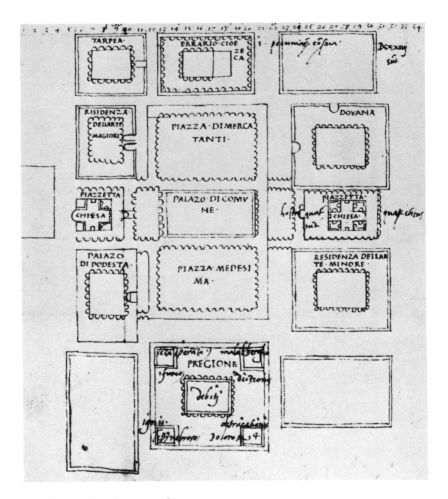

42. Filarete, *Treatise on Architecture,*
Piazza dei Mercanti; Florence, Biblioteca
Nazionale, Cod. Pal. 1411 (photo: Bib.
Naz.)

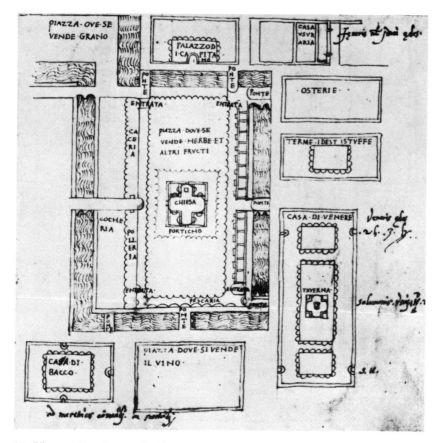

43. Filarete, *Treatise on Architecture,*
Marketplace; Florence, Biblioteca
Nazionale, Cod. Pal. 1411 (photo: Bib.
Naz.)

44. Vigevano, Piazza Ducale, looking
toward the Castello Sforzesco (photo:
Vigevano, Verga)

45. Vigevano, Piazza Ducale, looking
toward the cathedral (photo: Vigevano,
Verga)

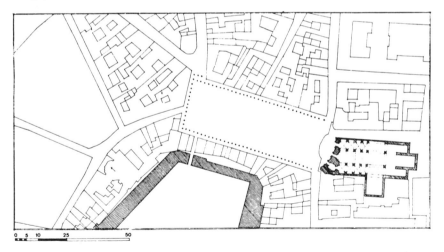

0 5 10   25   50

46. Vigevano, Piazza Ducale, ground
plan (after De Bernardi Ferrero)

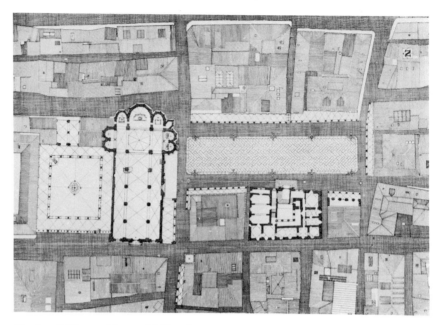

47. Ascoli Piceno, Piazza del Popolo,
ground plan

48. Pienza, Piazza, ground plan

49. Pienza, Piazza (photo: Florence,
Kunsthistorisches Institut)

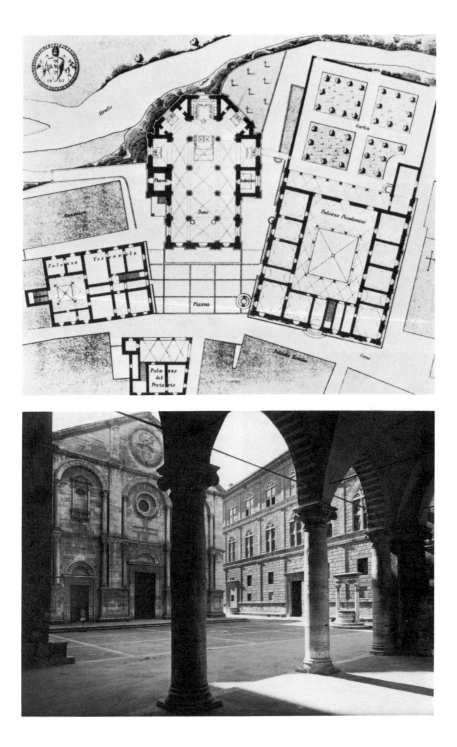

103

50. Ascoli Piceno, Piazza del Popolo, looking toward the church of San Francesco (photo: Ascoli Piceno, Terni)

51. Ascoli Piceno, Piazza del Popolo, looking toward the Palazzo Comunale (photo: Ascoli Piceno, Terni)

52. Florence, Piazza Santissima
Annunziata (photo: Florence, Pratesi)

53. Florence, Piazza Santissima Annunziata (photo: Florence, Tognoli)

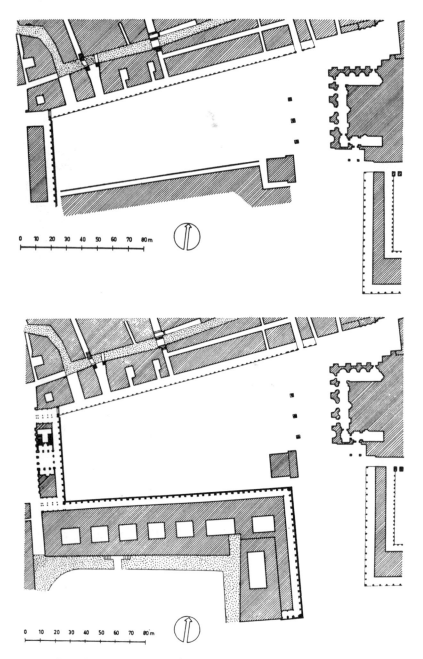

54. Venice, Piazza San Marco: *above,*
ground plan, about 1500; *below,*
present-day ground plan with the
Piazzetta

55. Venice, Piazza San Marco, aerial
view (photo: Bibliotheca Hertziana)

56. Gentile Bellini, *Procession of the
Holy Cross in the Piazza San Marco,
1496;* Venice, Accademia (photo:
Venice, Böhm)

58. Venice, Library of San Marco (photo: Alinari)

59. Venice, Piazzetta (photo: Venice,
B. V.)

CAPITOLII·SCIOGRAPHIA·EX·IPSO·EXEMPLARI·MICHAELIS·ANGELI·BONAROTI·A·STEPHANO·DVPERAC·PARISIENSI·ACCVRATE·DELINEATA ET·IN·LVCEM·AEDITA·ROMAE·ANNO·SALVTIS·∞DLXIX

60. Rome, Capitol, anonymous drawing, after 1549; Paris, Louvre (photo: Bibliotheca Hertziana)

61. Rome, Capitol, engraving by E. Dupérac, 1569 (photo: Bibliotheca Hertziana)

62. Rome, Capitol, ground plan, engraving, 1567 (photo: Bibliotheca Hertziana)

63. Rome, Capitol, drawing by Lieven
Cruyl, 1673 (photo: Florence, Gab. Fot.
Sopr.)

64. Rome, Farnese Palace, engraving
by Lafréry, 1549 (photo: Bibliotheca
Hertziana)

65. Rome, Farnese Palace (photo:
Rome, Gab. Fot. Naz.)

113

66. Bologna, Piazza Maggiore with the Municipal Palace and the Palace of the Podestà, *right* (photo: Bologna, Vera)

67. Bologna, Piazza Maggiore with the Portico dei Banchi (photo: Bologna, D. V. B.)

68. Bologna, Piazza Maggiore, drawing, eighteenth century

69. Vignola, design for the Portico dei Banchi; Berlin, Dahlem Museum, Kupferstich-Kabinett (photo: Berlin, Steinkopf)

115

70. Todi, Piazza Maggiore with the
Municipal Palace (photo: Todi, Ursini)

4
THE PIAZZA DUCALE IN VIGEVANO: A PRINCELY FORUM OF THE LATE FIFTEENTH CENTURY

The Piazza Ducale in Vigevano was built between 1492 and 1494, a remarkably short time.[1] The patron was Ludovico Maria Sforza il Moro, during these years regent of the duchy of Milan for his nephew, Gian Galeazzo Sforza. Upon Gian Galeazzo's death in October 1494, Il Moro succeeded him to the dukedom. The square in Vigevano is closely related to a large castle[2] which had been used earlier by the Visconti as an occasional residence outside Milan, thirty-five kilometers away. The castle, seized and partly destroyed by local residents after the death of the last Visconti in 1447, was restored by the new duke, Francesco Sforza.[3] His son Ludovico Maria, who was born there in 1451, rebuilt and enlarged it.[4] There he received Charles VIII of France in 1494, and a little later the Emperor Maximilian, who through his wife Bianca Maria, a niece of Il Moro, was related to the Sforza family.

The following essay will propose a reconstruction of the square, which was much altered by later rebuilding and additions, and will seek to define its importance for the history of urbanism. Further, the questions of authorship and the distinctive relationship of the Renaissance to antiquity as revealed by the plan of the piazza will be examined.

The square (Figs. 46, 71, 72) is 134 meters long and 48 meters wide, including the bordering arcades. Today there are twelve bays on the short west side and thirty three on each of the long sides (shown in Fig. 72). The short side on the east of the square is taken up by the baroque facade of the Cathedral of Sant' Ambrogio (Fig. 71). It is immediately clear from the modern appearance of the square that the polychrome decoration of the three older facades (Fig. 73) results from a historicizing restoration of about 1900. The painter Casimiro Ottone, who performed the restoration,[5] removed a coat of paint applied in 1757, when the facades were

Published in German as "Die Piazza Ducale von Vigevano: Ein fürstliches Forum des späten 15. Jahrhunderts," in *Kunsthistorische Forschungen: Otto Pächt zu Ehren* (Salzburg, 1972), pp. 243–257; published in Italian as "La Piazza Ducale di Vigevano: Un foro princepesco del tardo Quattrocento," in *Studi Bramanteschi: Atti del congresso internazionale*, 1970, Milan, Urbino, Rome (1974), pp. 205–221 whitewashed and the windows set off by pink frames.[6] Under the rococo layers were found the remains of the fifteenth-century decoration, which, although recorded in watercolors (Fig. 76), was used only to a minor extent as a model for the restoration.

The architectural form of the square does not correspond to that of the later fifteenth century either. The arcades, the portions of the castle visible from the square, and the high tower that dominates the square have all been altered. The castle was used as a barracks for artillery units beginning in 1860, when Lombardy joined the new Kingdom of Italy. In a remodelling of the barracks in 1872, a high wall was raised on the left side of the tower behind the arcades of the square.[7] The nine bays in front of the wall, on the other hand, were erected in the late seventeenth century. The original form of this side of the square can be seen in a ground plan of 1626 (Fig. B). In spite of the somewhat awkward representation, it can be observed that the difference in level of almost 7 meters between the court of the castle and the square was equalized by means of a ramp leading from the ground floor of the tower to the square.

According to the plan of 1626, the tower and the adjacent bays of the north side of the castle were fully visible from the square. Thus, as the center of the "open" section of this side, the tower dominated the prospect of the square in a totally different way than it does today. The 1626 plan further shows that the short, west side of the square, which now has twelve bays, extended all the way to the castle and had at least fifteen, and possibly even seventeen bays;[8] the "missing" bays are partly preserved in the later construction (see reconstruction, Fig. C).

An old street, the Via del Popolo, runs into the short side of the square from the west, and its opening is bridged by a double arcade (Fig. 74). On the north side of the opening there are now six bays, while on the south side toward the castle there are four. If one adds the bays that were eliminated in the seventeenth century (necessarily disregarding the unknown shape of the last bay adjoining the castle) there would be seven— or possibly nine—arcades on the south side of the street opening, as against the six on the north. Thus the street opening would have given the optical impression of being in the center of the short side.

The last three arcades of the long, north side of the square also bridge a street opening (Fig. 75). Here again changes in the original condition can be seen: the capitals of the two columns differ from those on the north side (Fig. 77), and are obviously a nineteenth-century inter-

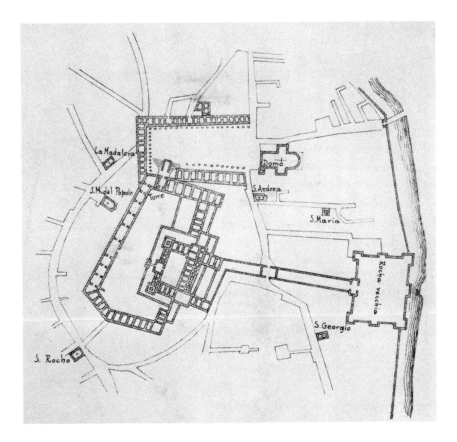

B. Vigevano, Castle and Piazza, ground
plan of 1626

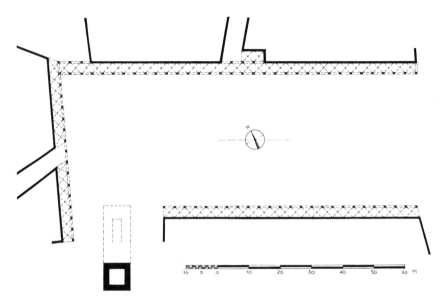

C. Vigevano, Piazza, reconstruction of
the original plan

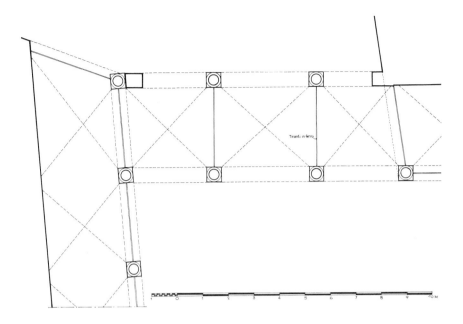

Tiranti in ferro

D. Vigevano, Piazza, passage at the
northwest corner, ground plan

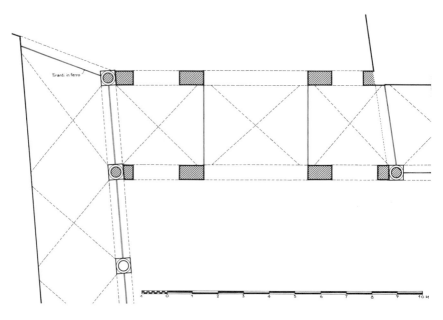

E. Vigevano, Piazza, passage at the
northwest corner, reconstruction of the
original plan

pretation of a Quattrocento style. The outer wall of the passageway rests on three arches, of which the westernmost is supported on one side by a column and on the other by a pier (Fig. 78). On the easternmost bay of the passageway is a projection of the wall. The three arches vary in breadth and curvature. These irregularities could be explained readily if one were to assume that the present arches result from a rebuilding in which the original piers were replaced by columns.

An examination of the inner side of the passageway confirms this assumption. One of the watercolors recording its condition after the removal of the rococo paint and before the modern restoration, shows this portion of the piazza facade (Fig. 76).[9] Comparing the watercolor with the present condition (Fig. 75), one sees both the problems that confronted the restorer Ottone and the problematic outcome of his decisions. Instead of the original piers, he found the columns of the earlier restoration, which had to be adjusted somehow to the painted pilasters of the original decoration. One can see further that originally the piers had carried the vaults over the passageway. Precisely when they were replaced by the present columns is not indicated in the sources,[10] but the form of the capitals suggests that they were made in the middle of the nineteenth century.

The key to a reconstruction of the original condition lies in the depiction of the old decoration, from which it appears that the middle bay was somewhat wider and the side passages notably narrower than today (Figs. D and E). The openings in the upper story of the square facade evidently were cut in modern times. These alterations are easily explained: in the upper story they were required by the new apartments, and on the ground level the lateral gateways, probably intended originally just for pedestrians, were widened to admit vehicles. All this could be accomplished best by making the three bays in question conform to the system of the rest of the facades.

A detailed reconstruction of the triumphal arch painted on the facade over the passageway is hindered by the fact that there is no evidence for the original height of the side passages. But obviously this triumphal arch is closely related to the facade of Sant' Andrea in Mantua, designed two decades earlier. Common to both systems is the articulation and proportion of the colossal order of pilasters, the absence of the projecting freestanding columns characteristic of ancient triumphal arches, and the relationship of the low and narrow side passages to the high broad central one.

In addition to this three-bay triumphal arch, there was another one with only one bay, which bridged the entrance to the Via del Popolo on the short side of the square. As the "new" capital of the column now standing under the arch shows, neither the column nor the two arcades supported by it belong to the original project.[11] For the renovation of the painted pilasters above the arcades the restorer Ottone had fewer clues to guide him than he had for the triple arch: the proportion of the pilasters and their relationship to the painted arch give an effect of dubious validity. Yet the similarities between them and the pilasters of the triple arch indicate that the restorer found vestiges of older pilasters. Apparently, however, the newly-painted arch is too high. An article published soon after the renovation criticized the escutcheon over the center for its heraldic or epigrammatic faults.[12] It would seem that here the painter took numerous liberties, and one can assume that he dealt in the same manner with the architectural system. If the height of the arch were reduced, the escutcheon would fall somewhat lower and fit into its proper place in the attic zone. The coat of arms and the inscription must have had the same relative position as they had over the triple arch and, as there, the bottom of the escutcheon must have overlapped the frieze of the painted entablature.

The significance of the two triumphal arches in the overall scheme of the piazza can be read clearly from the ground plan (Fig. C). The single arch at the center of the short, west side lay on the long axis of the square; the triple arch of the long, north side corresponded to the tower directly opposite and to the visible parts of the castle facade. When entering the square through the triple arch, one was confronted with the ramp leading up to the portal of the tower. Conversely, when descending from the castle through the portal to the square, one faced the triumphal arch now concealed by later buildings. A marble plaque still exists over the portal of the tower with a long Latin inscription, dated 1492, which informs us about the design and significance of the piazza:

After quieting external and internal disorders, Ludovico Maria Sforza Visconti, in the reign of his nephew Gian Galeazzo, made the impoverished land of Vigevano fruitful by diverting rivers, remade this castle, the seat of preceding princes, into a beautiful residence, enlarged it by additions, and fortified it with a magnificent tower. By laying and paving roads, he turned the old, squalid residential quarters of the populace into an ornament of the community. Finally, after the old buildings surrounding the forum had been torn down, he made the square more beautiful by enlarging it and surrounding it with arcades. In the year of grace 1492.[13]

This text leaves no doubt that the piazza was the creation of Il Moro. We know from the sources that in April and May 1492 Ludovico instructed the town council to survey the houses and stores destined for destruction.[14] To compensate the owners, the taxes owed for years 1493 and 1494 were assumed by the state.[15] In August 1494, the Ferrarese ambassador reported to his court that "Ludovico is trying very hard to beautify Vigevano and to make it into a city [the town had not yet been granted a charter]; in the vicinity of the castle he has torn down a rather wide street of houses to make way for a beautiful, wide, and very long square with arcades, columns, and arches surrounded by shops: when it is completed it will be a beautiful and magnificent thing."[16]

As the sources and inscription tell us, the old market street,[17] the municipal palace,[18] and other buildings were sacrificed to the new piazza.[19] However, neither the artistic nor the political significance of the plan is explained adequately by ascribing the work of demolition and the vastness of the new square solely to the architectural ambitions of a Renaissance prince. And it does not suffice to point out that this is the first example since antiquity of a piazza built in one campaign and surrounded by uniform arcades.[20]

We have mentioned that, after the death of the last Visconti duke in August 1447, the people of Vigevano appropriated the old castle. At that time the government of the newly constituted Republica Ambrosiana in Milan occupied and razed the ducal castle at Porta Giovia.[21] On 4 October 1447, an agreement made between the Republica Ambrosiana and the free commune of Vigevano[22] stipulated that the castle of Vigevano with its church of Sant' Ambrogio "shall again become the property of the commune as it has been since ancient times."[23]

The new municipal council of Vigevano now proclaimed their hope that God might preserve their happily won freedom for eternity;[24] but it was a rather brief eternity. The republican authority in Milan proved unable to maintain internal stability; state finances and the distribution of food fell into hopeless disorder; and famines and numerous executions are reported in the chronicles.[25] Three years later the people rejoiced when the new duke, Francesco Sforza, entered Milan. Shortly before, he had captured the stubbornly defended town of Vigevano and had established himself at the castle. The castle had been promised expressly to the commune by the Republica Ambrosiana in 1447. But in the terms of surrender concluded on 13 October 1449 between Francesco Sforza, then still Count of Pavia, and the commune of Vigevano, it was mentioned only insofar as the burghers who had established residence in the moat were given permission to remain.[26] Only a few small buildings could have been involved in this arrangement; it was apparently taken for granted that the castle itself would belong to the new ruler.

The 1492 inscription on the tower, in which Ludovico Maria speaks of quieting internal and external disorders, of the enlargement and fortification of the castle, and of the building of the new square, can be understood fully only in connection with the events of 1447–1450. The significance of the square, for which the town was forced to pay, is tied closely to that of the neighboring ducal castle. Indeed, the piazza is, as the inscription tells us, an ornament of the community; yet the height of the tower and the tenor of the inscription leave little doubt that the square, conceived by the prince and dominated by the tower, forms an integral part of the princely residence. The freedom of the commune, proclaimed in 1447, had been replaced already in 1449 by a new civic order, which a little more than four decades later received its exact architectural expression in the relationship of castle to piazza. It is not by chance that the square was named the Piazza Ducale; usually the municipal squares in Lombardy were called either Piazza del Popolo or simply Piazza Grande.

As a rule, the medieval municipal palaces in the free communes of the Po Valley stand either between two squares, as in Padua and Vicenza, or they project on three sides into the square, as in Piacenza. Nothing is known of the appearance and site of the medieval town hall of Vigevano, which was torn down to make room for the new piazza. That the community received the relatively large subsidy of 1,000 ducats from Il Moro for the new building[27] would indicate that the old one was sizable.

The new town hall is located at the center of the long, north side of the square. Only the municipal coat of arms on the facade distinguishes it from the adjacent buildings on either side.[28] If we assume that the destroyed building, like surviving examples of the type elsewhere, was partially or completely freestanding, thereby symbolizing the independence of the commune, then the incorporation of the new Palazzo Comunale in the facade of the piazza had a specific, political significance: it bore witness to the end of communal independence.

As has been stated, the piazza of Vigevano is the first Renaissance example of a square surrounded by uniform arcades and built in a single campaign. It is surely no accident that in the tower inscription the site is designated by the classical term *forum* and not by the late Latin-medieval term *platea,* which survives as *piazza* or *place.* The text of the inscription corresponds exactly to the architectural form, which can be understood only as an imitation of a Roman forum. The ancient type of square, however, was known to the Renaissance exclusively through a literary source, namely the treatise of Vitruvius. Vitruvius's description of the forum is repeated almost verbatim in Alberti's *Ten Books on Architecture.* The editio princeps of Alberti's treatise of 1485 appears in the 1503 catalogue of Leonardo da Vinci's books.[29] Leonardo worked for Ludovico il Moro in both Milan and Vigevano. Further, we can assume that the 1486 editio princeps of Vitruvius was known among the humanists of the Milanese court.[30]

That the piazza of Vigevano represents a fundamentally new formal concept is evident from a comparison of it with the piazza constructed in Pienza about 1460 or with the squares for the ideal city of Sforzinda, designed by Filarete for Francesco Sforza, the father of Il Moro. In Pienza the four principal buildings of the town—the cathedral, the town hall, the palaces of the bishop and of the Piccolomini—all stand on the square.[31] Loggias appear here only on the ground floor of the Palazzo Comunale, a medieval type of town hall commonly found in Tuscany and widespread throughout northern Italy and Germany. Likewise, the facades of the other three buildings conform to respective types of Quattrocento building. Although they were all erected at once, the buildings on the square in Pienza are thus heterogeneous and not, as in Vigevano, homogeneous.

Filarete's project for the municipal square of Sforzinda is known only from a ground plan.[32] The Palazzo del Comune stands in the center of the Piazza del Mercato (Fig. 42), as it does in the medieval towns of Lombardy. To this extent the project is quite traditional. However, another of Filarete's squares in Sforzinda, the fruit and vegetable market-place (Fig. 43), does anticipate one of the characteristics of the piazza in Vigevano by being surrounded on all sides by loggias. Filarete's text re-peatedly mentions Alberti, and it is possible that the loggias around the "piazza dove si vende herbe et altri fructi" reflect Alberti's description of the ancient forum. But since a church stands in the center of his vegetable market, Filarete here could not have had in mind the open space of the ancient forum any more than for his plan of the municipal square.

Thus the new distinctive formal aspects of the piazza in Vigevano are the analogous treatment of its three facades, the uniform loggias on the ground floor with their stores and workshops, and the open center of the square, made possible by incorporating the town hall into one of the sides of the piazza. All these features are found in Vitruvius and in the description of the ancient forum which Alberti took from him.[33] The connection seems all the more indisputable because the word *forum* appears in the inscription commemorating the square's founding in 1492. The striking parallels indicate that the wording of the inscription was consciously based on the texts of Vitruvius and Alberti:

INSCRIPTION OF 1492 ON THE TOWER OF VIGEVANO—
Ludovicus Maria Sfortia . . . dirutis . . . *circa forum* veteribus edificiis *aream ampliavit ac porticibus circumductis exornavit*
ALBERTI (*Ten Books on Architecture*, VIII, 6)—
Forum Græci quadratum constituebant, *porticibus amplissimis* et duplicibus *circumibant*, columnis et trabibus lapideis *ornabant*[34]
VITRUVIUS, 5:1—
Græci in quadrato *amplissimis* et duplicibus *porticibus fora* constituunt *crebrisque columnis et lapideis aut marmoreis epistyliis adornant* (italics mine)

Ludovico il Moro had marble plaques with Latin inscriptions set into his other buildings in Vigevano as well. The Sforzesca, Ludovico's model farm outside the town gates, has two texts by the great Latinist, Ermolao Barbaro, which describe the purpose of the estate and the blessings of *Agricultura*.[35] Characteristic antique *topoi* crop up in their formulations also. Barbaro was no longer in Lombardy in 1492, so the text on the tower of Vigevano was composed by another humanist at the Sforza court.[36] Ludovico and his learned entourage would not have had difficulty recognizing the allusions it contained.

That around 1500 ancient architecture was regarded as exemplary needs no emphasizing. In Vigevano the example was not an ancient building— there were after all no longer any ancient fora to be seen—but rather the text of Vitruvius. While the conception of the square was determined by the literary exemplar of the Vitruvian forum, the masons who carved the columns and capitals worked in the characteristic Lombard manner of the late Quattrocento.

When Julius II began the rebuilding of St. Peter's in Rome, a medal
was struck which depicts Bramante's project for the new church with the
inscription: TEMPLI PETRI INSTAURACIO. Were a similar medal to exist
for the piazza of Vigevano, it could be inscribed: FORI VIGLEVANI
INSTAURACIO. According to Isidore of Seville, "ædificatio nova constructio
est, instauratio vero quod reparatur ad instar prioris."[37] Thus, in contrast to
aedificatio, "new building," *instauratio* means a reconstruction after an
older or earlier model. Obviously, neither Julius II nor his architect
Bramante thought that the Constantinian church of St. Peter's looked like
Bramante's project on the medal. The latter is, rather, an *instauratio* of
an ideal *Templum Petri*. In much the same way, the piazza of Vigevano
can be taken as the *instauratio* of an ideal forum "all'antica," even if,
surely, no one really thought that the forum of the ancient Viglevanum
looked like the square of 1492.

In Alberti's treatise the description of the ancient forum is followed by a
list of specifications for the proportions and details of piazza facades. From
the wording it is clear that Alberti is thinking of modern buildings.[38]
Immediately after there follows a passage on ancient triumphal arches
in which their decoration is described and their form is derived, on the
authority of Tacitus, from the city gate. As we can see here and in many
other passages in Alberti's text, modern practice can no more be separated
from the picture of antiquity than it can be in the image on the medal
of St. Peter's.

It is Alberti's passage on the triumphal arch which bears most directly
on the municipal square of Vigevano:

Sed quod forosque . . . maiorem in modum exornent sunt arcus ad fauces
viarum statuti. Est enim arcus veluti perpetuo patens porta . . . quod
opus id celeberrimo staret loco, ea re illic captas ab hoste exuvias et notas
victoriae deponebant. Inde coeptus ornari arcus est, adiectique et tituli et
statuae et historia. Arcum aptissime astruemus illic, ubi via in plateam aut
forum terminabit. Et praesertim via regia (sic enim appello viam quae
intra urbem omnium dignissima est). Atqui arcus . . . tris habebit itiones
pervias: media, quam miles; hinc vero atque hinc, quibus matres suique
victorem exercitum redeuntem ad patrios deos consalutandos comitentur et
orantibus plaudent ac congratulantur. . . .[39]

The arches over the gateways to the piazza of Vigevano span the two
most important streets leading to the square. Their painted "tituli et
statuae et historia" (coats of arms and devices) are the triumphal "exuviae

et notae" of the Sforza duke.[40] Here the image of antiquity, topical political statement, and practical function have been fused in a new architectural conception of the forum, and the painted triumphal arch appears as an integral part of this conception.[41]

The identity of the designer of the piazza cannot be determined conclusively from the literary sources and the original documents. At the time in question, Leonardo da Vinci and Bramante were working at the castles of the Sforzas in Milan, Pavia, and Vigevano; their presence in Vigevano in 1494 is documented.[42] On 16 February Bramante had twelve columns transported from the Certosa of Pavia to Vigevano;[43] a document of 24 February gives him authority to quarry marble and to have it brought to Vigevano.[44] Two notes written by Leonardo are dated in Vigevano on 2 February "alla Sforzesca," and 20 March at the "Vigne di Vigevano."[45] Meanwhile, about this time the work on the piazza was drawing to a close: in July 1494 it was paved, and in September the vaults of the arcades were whitewashed. From several documents of 1492 we learn that the surveying of the condemned houses and the supervision of building activities were in the hands of Ambrogio da Corte, a high-ranking engineer, frequently mentioned in documents in connection with other buildings of the court.[46] But the plan for Vigevano scarcely can be ascribed to him.

On the contrary, there are many arguments which favor assigning the 1492 design of the piazza to Bramante. It was Bramante who, a decade and a half later, laid the cornerstone for the new St. Peter's, which called for the razing of the Constantinian basilica. His Cortile del Belvedere is still one of the most imposing architectural complexes in Italy. The piazza in Vigevano shows the same characteristics that distinguish Bramante's Roman works: extraordinary dimensions; planning at once grand and reckless, which stands apart from everything else in its time; and the assimilation rather than slavish imitation of ancient ideas. To this we may add the distinctive architectural decoration of the two painted triumphal arches with their illusionistic perspective,[47] which have their exact counterparts in the frescoes with which Bramante began his work in Lombardy.[48] As already mentioned, the articulation of the triple arch at Vigevano indicates a knowledge of Alberti's facade of Sant' Andrea in Mantua; other buildings by Bramante also show Alberti's influence.

Finally, there is one detail of the triple arch, as F. Graf Wolff Metternich has shown, which in Lombard architecture of the late

Quattrocento is found only in the work of Bramante: the Corinthian, horizontally divided basket capital, which is a literal interpretation of a passage in Vitruvius. The same capital appears in the engraving of 1481 by Bernardo Prevedari, labeled "Bramante fecit."[49]

Both the conception of the square and these characteristic architectural details demonstrate that the project, whose scale is unique in the Quattrocento, was the work of Bramante. Its execution could not have been supervised entirely by Bramante, for we know that in December 1493, that is, while work was still in progress in Vigevano, Ludovico il Moro instructed his agents in Florence and Rome to look for the architect because "he is now needed here [in Vigevano]."[50]

Surely, it can be taken for granted that Leonardo and Bramante discussed the project when they were together at the court of the Sforzas even though no specific evidence has so far been found in Leonardo's extensive notes and drawings that he was involved in the planning and decoration of the piazza.[51]

The later history of the piazza can only be outlined here. Its creator, Ludovico il Moro, assumed the title of Duke of Milan on the death of his nephew in 1494, but his rule lasted only until 1499, not very much longer, that is, than the Republica Ambrosiana of 1447. He died in 1508, a prisoner of the French. In the following three decades, Milan was a bone of contention between the great powers of France and the Hapsburgs and changed hands repeatedly; two of Il Moro's sons also ruled as dukes for a short time. In 1534, following the death of Francesco II Sforza, the old imperial fief of Milan was repossessed by Emperor Charles V. In 1743, after two hundred years of Hapsburg rule, Vigevano together with the western part of the dukedom was ceded to Savoy by Maria Theresa.

Consequently, by 1500, Il Moro's coat of arms and devices on the piazza had lost their meaning, and when Lombardy was taken over by Charles V the castle lost its function as residence. The conception of the piazza as the symbol of a political structure and of the relationship between a prince and his subjects was without purpose when the castle and town were administered by the functionary of a ruler residing in Madrid, Vienna, or Turin. But the community lived on. In 1532, it was given a charter as a city by the last of the Sforzas—a farewell gift of the dynasty, as it were. At the same time Vigevano became a bishopric. In 1533, a new cathedral was begun at the eastern end of the square to replace the old Church of Sant' Ambrogio.[52] It took eighty years, until 1612, before the cathedral could be dedicated; in contrast, the construction of the entire piazza had required only two.

Another seventy years passed before the new church, under the Spanish bishop, Juan Caramuel de Lobkowitz, received its concave facade (Figs. 71, 79), which gives the piazza its characteristic appearance today.[53] The design was conceived by the bishop himself, a highly educated amateur architect, who installed a printing press in the episcopal palace; among the many books published there was the treatise *Architectura civil Recta y Obliqua considerada y dibuxada en el Templo de Jerusalem.*

The facade of the cathedral was erected in front of the church and its adjacent street; but neither the long axis of the square nor the center of the facade is in line with the central axis of the church. Of the four "portals," only three lead into the church; the fourth bridges the opening of the street (Fig. 46). Thanks to this ingenious arrangement, which is a variation on the motif of the street openings at the opposite end of the square, the facade fills the entire east end of the piazza.

With the erection of the facade, Caramuel removed the ramp that led from the castle to the square.[54] The castle's new function as a garrison no longer called for its visual connection with the piazza. For this reason, the loggias of the piazza facades were now extended in front of the walls of the castle, which had been exposed originally to the square. In the process the architectural forms of the late fifteenth century were followed precisely (Fig. 79)[55]—a notable example of conservation during the Baroque period. Only the crozier on the capitals identifies Bishop Caramuel as the builder (Fig. 80). With the disappearance of its ground floor behind the piazza arcades, the tower lost its original significance as the dominant element of the piazza. The cathedral, now the most important building on the square, filled the vacuum left by the disappearance of the castle and tower.

In this way the Piazza Ducale became the Piazza del Duomo.[56] And yet, by adopting the existing architectural scheme for the new arcades in front of the castle, the seventeenth-century bishop demonstrated his approval of the piazza's original form. With the erection of the cathedral facade the original emphasis placed on the axial relationship of triumphal arch and castle entrance lost its formal significance as well. It was only logical, in consequence, to create an overall, unified scheme and make the formerly "irregular" parts conform to the rest of the square.

The conception of the Sforza forum as a "piazza-salone"[57] has survived all the reconstructions and political changes. For the present inhabitants of Vigevano and its visitors, the free space of the Piazza Ducale is no less an "ornament of the community" than it was for its builder and his architect who created it in 1492 "ad civilem lautitiam." As a work of art it has long outlived the transitory political message bound to the person of its creator.[58]

Notes

1. More complete details on the layout of the castle are in F. Malaguzzi Valeri, *Lodovico* 1: pp. 646ff. Documents are in Colombo, "Piazza Ducale," pp. 248ff.

2. On the castle see Galileo Barucci, *Castello,* passim; the best photograph is in Vittorio R. Ramella, "Castello," pp. 72–73.

3. See Colombo, "Vigevano," pp. 333ff.

4. See Malaguzzi Valeri, *Lodovico* 1: p. 654.

5. On the restoration see Colombo, "Armi e leggenda," Malaguzzi Valeri, *Lodovico* 2: pp. 171 ff.

6. See Colombo, "Piazza Ducale," p. 249. This condition is shown in our Fig. 79.

7. See Barucci, *Castello,* p. 32, #1, and Malaguzzi Valeri, *Lodovico* 1: p. 652.

8. The ground plan of 1626—illustrated in Malaguzzi Valeri, *Lodovico* 2: Fig. 184, and Barucci, *Castello,* p. 34—which shows twelve bays is demonstrably inaccurate: for instance, in place of the thirty-three bays on the long side, which is still in its original condition, the plan indicates only nineteen arcades. Berghoef, "Origines," Fig. 17, reconstructs the narrow end in question with seventeen arcades, the number obtained if one assumes

that the last arcade of the piazza facade adjoined the outer wall of the castle. In our reconstruction (Fig. C), only the fifteen arcades that can be ascertained beyond a doubt have been drawn in. In the reconstruction of Daria De Bernardi Ferrero, "Caramuel," Fig. 21, the arcades removed from the west end in the seventeenth century are not taken into account.

9. See Colombo, "Piazza Ducale," Fig. on p. 251, hereafter our Fig. 76.

10. Colombo seems to assume that the change was made in the seventeenth century ("Armi e leggenda," p. 181, #2).

11. *Ibid.,* #10.

12. *Ibid.,* pp. 180ff.

13. Lvdovicvs Maria Sfortia Vicecomes principatv Joanni Galeacio Nepoti ab exteris et intestinis motibvs stabilito postea qvam sqvallentes agros Viglevanenses immissis flvminibvs fertiles fecit ad volvptuarios seccessvs in hac arce veteres principvm edes reformavit et novis circvmedificatis speciosa etiam turri mvnivit popvli qvoqve habitationes sitv et sqvalore occvpatas stratis et expeditis per vrbem viis ad civilem lavticiam redegit dirvtis etiam circa forvm veteribvs edificiis aream ampliavit ac porticibvs circvmdvctis in hanc speciem exornavit anno a

salvte christiana nonagesimo secvndo svpra millesimvm et quvadrigentesimvm. The text of the inscription "sopra la Porta principale d'esso Castello, sotto la Torre, e in capo della Piazza dei Mercanti" is in Egidio Sacchetti, *Vigevano*, pp. 99ff.; see also Pietro G. Biffignandi, *Memorie* 1: p. 227; Barucci, *Castello*, p. 31.

14. See Colombo, "Piazza Ducale," p. 248.

15. *Ibid.*, p. 249; at the end of 1494 the communal tax on horses was abolished permanently.

16. The ambassador's letter is published in Malaguzzi Valeri, *Lodovico* 1: pp. 654–655: "Luni passata venissemo la sira al tardi a Viglievano el quale è un bello et grosso castello de circuito, ma a mio iudicio non tropo honorevole ni anche tropo civile ne de giente ni anche de edificij. Li sono bene alcune strate assai large et che da poco in qua sono stà selegate de codali osia giaroni, ma de case poi non li è grassa. Lo Ill.mo S.re Ludovico fa ogni reforzo per redurlo a civilitade et anche a nome de citade et dove era una bella strada larga apresso el castello, ha facto butare per terra tute le case da ogni lato et fa fare una bella piazza molto longa e larga cum portici cum columne et volti et botege da ogni lato che serà una bella cossa e honorevole quando la serà fornita. El castello autem ha un grande circuito et è in forteza et dentro li sono allozamenti assai." (See also Bruschi, *Bramante*, pp. 804ff.)

17. See note 16. According to a late sixteenth-century chronicle, the piazza was "antica di lunghezza come ora la nuova . . . anzi non era piazza, ma contrada, perchè ivi

si vendeva; e mercantesca era detta piazza, e sotto essi portici erano botteghe . . ." (C. Nubilonio, *Cronaca di Vigevano* [Turin, 1892], pp. 250ff.; hereafter Nubilonio, *Cronaca*).

18. See note 13; A. Colombo, *L'alloggio del Podestà di Vigevano e il Palazzo del Comune nel secolo XV* (Mortara-Vigevano, 1901). (This work was not available to the author.)

19. The old Palazzo di Giustizia was also destroyed (see Nubilonio, *Cronaca*, p. 250, and Biffignandi, *Memorie*, 1: p. 195; the latter (p. 228) says the same as Nubilonio: ". . . ancora al presente veggonsi alcune sotterranee cantine, le quali si estendono sino alla metà della piazza, antichi fondamenti delle case . . . demolite"). The length of the piazza of 1492 was determined by the old church and the old street block that led through the triple arch to the castle; Nubilonio proves that the length of the new piazza coincides with the ancient *contrada* (*Cronaca*, pp. 250ff.). In contrast, the width has been definitely enlarged, as is evident from the ground plan of the arbitrarily sheared off houses along the south side (our Fig. 46) and from the existence of foundations of older buildings beneath the pavement of the present piazza.

20. See Chap. 3; Giovannoni, *Saggi*, p. 278; Bruschi, *Bramante*, p. 647; L. Mumford does not do justice to the facts when he sees in Vigevano an example of city planning by military engineers (*The City in History* [London, 1966], p. 442).

21. See F. Cognasso, *Storia di Milano*

(Milan, 1955), 6: p. 401 (hereafter Cognasso, *Storia*).

22. See Colombo, "Vigevano," pp. 342f.

23. *Ibid.*, pp. 334, 346. The relevant passage in the agreement reads: ". . . Castellatium vetus Viglevani in quo est ecclesia sancti Ambrosii patroni dictae terrae sit, et esse debeat, Comunis Viglevani, et remaneat in potestate dicti Comunis, et fuit principium dictae terrae, nec in eo in perpetuum aliquid innovari possit contra voluntatem Comunis Viglevani" (A. Colombo, *Bollettino Società Pavese di Storia Patria* 3 [1903]: p. 491).

24. "Ex bona libertate, quam utinam deus semper manuteneat" (Colombo, "Vigevano," p. 334).

25. A detailed description is found in Cognasso, *Storia,* pp. 430ff.

26. ". . . quod hedifitia facta in fosso Castelatii circum circa remaneant prout sint. Et in eo hedificari possit ad libitum voluntatis eorum, qui habent sedimina, quia tempore . . . Ducis [Filippo Maria Visconti] non prohibebatur hedificare . . ." (Colombo, "Vigevano," p. 315).

27. See Colombo, "Piazza Ducale," p. 249.

28. See Colombo, "Armi e leggenda," pp. 181ff. From the minutes of the town council meeting of 21 July, 1494, we learn that Il Moro instructed the community to paint, in addition to the communal coat-of-arms, the "arma ducalia et Illmi D. D. Ludovici Marie Sfortie . . . super pariete palacii anterioris . . . in omni pulchritudine" on the new town hall (*ibid.*, p. 182).

29. See L. Reti, "The Two Unpublished Manuscripts of Leonardo da Vinci

in the Biblioteca Nacional of Madrid, II", *The Burlington Magazine* 110 (1968): p. 81. The passages in Vitruvius and Alberti are given here on p. 76.

30. See G. Scaglia, Review of C. Maltese, *Trattati di architettura, ingegneria e arte militare di Francesco di Giorgio Martini*, in *The Art Bulletin,* 53 (1970): p. 441.

31. See "Pius II," pp. 105ff.; and Carli, *Pienza,* p. 46.

32. Concerning this, Filarete's text says: ". . . voglio fare in quella [piazza] de'mercatanti il palazzo de'mercatanti e dove ha a stare la ragione [the Palazzo di Giustizia] e nell'altra piazza o vuoi dire mercato dove molte cose si venderà voglio fare il palazzo del capitano del popolo . . ." (*Treatise,* II: Book 8, fol. 61 *recto*); drawings of the piazza project are in *Cod. Pal.* 1411, Biblioteca Nazionale, Florence, hereafter our Figs. 42, 43).

33. Alberti "non fa che esporre le norme di Vitruvio" (G. Orlandi, *Leon Battista Alberti, l'Architettura* [Milan, 1966], p. 715).

34. See chap. 3, pp. 56–57, and Bruschi; ". . . l'idea di una piazza fiancheggiata da portici deriva con evidenza dalla volontà umanistica di riferirsi al tipo del *forum* romano" (*Bramante,* p. 648).

35. The texts are published in Biffignandi, *Memorie,* 1: pp. 223ff., and in Malaguzzi Valeri, *Lodovico* 1: p. 668, #1 with Italian translation; see also L. H. Heydenreich, *Bollettino Centro Internazionale di Studi d'Architettura 'Andrea Palladio'* 11 (1969): pp. 14ff. On Ermolao Barbaro, Venetian envoy to the Milanese court in 1488–89, see V. Branca, "Ermolao Barbaro e

l'umanesimo veneziano," *Umanesimo Europeo e Umanesimo Veneziano* (Florence, 1963), pp. 193ff.

36. According to Barucci, *Castello,* p.
30, Barbaro also composed the inscription over the main portal of
the castle: Ludovicus Maria Sfortia
Divorum Francisci Sfortiae et
Biancae Mariae Filius et Barri Dux
hunc amenissimum locum carissimi
nepotis joannis galeatii ducis secessi-
bus exornavit. The antique topos
amœnissimum locum is also in the
inscription above the stables of the
castle: Ludovicus Mar. Sfort. Vicec.
Divor. Francisci et Mariae Biancae
F. Barri Dux ne quid in ameniss.
secessu disideretur purpuratis equis
cariss. Nepotis Jo. Galeacii Ducis
Mli. ab fundamentis absolvit.
(Barucci, *Castello,* p. 31; and Malaguzzi Valeri, *Lodovico* 2: p. 162
with Fig. of the plaque).

37. *Etymologiarum,* W. M. Lindsay, ed.
(Oxford, 1911), 19.10.1.

38. *Ten Books on Architecture,* VIII,
cap. 6. The use of the future tense
is characteristic—". . . at nos
forum etiam probabimus"; or
". . . latitudo quidem erit quanta
et columnis altitudo."

39. "But nothing can be a greater Ornament . . . than arches at the entrance of the Streets; an Arch being
indeed nothing else but a Gate
standing continually open . . .
[The arch] was adorned with
spoils which [the ancients] won
from their Enemies, and the Ensigns
of their Victories. To these beginnings it was that Arches owed
their trophies, Inscriptions, Statues
and Relieves. A very proper situation for an Arch is where a Street
joins into a Square, and especially
in the Royal Street, by which

Name I understand the most emi-
nent in the City. An Arch, like a
Bridge, should have no less than
three open Passages: That in the
Middle for the Soldiers to return
through in Triumph to pay their
Devotions to their paternal Gods,
and the two Side ones for the
Matrons and Citizens to go out to
meet and welcome them Home"
(*Ten Books on Architecture,*
J. Leoni, trans. [London, 1955],
VIII, 6, p. 174).

40. An explanation of the inscription
and the devices is found in Colombo, "Armi e leggenda," pp.
180ff, and Malaguzzi Valeri, *Lodovico* 2: p. 171. The painted por-
trait medallions of the ruling duke
and duchess, Gian Galeazzo and
Isabella, on the triumphal arch of
the Via del Popolo disappeared
during the restoration, as did the
portraits of Ludovico il Moro and
Beatrice d'Este, which were still
visible in 1909 beside the inscription on the tower (see Barucci,
Castello, p. 32, and Malaguzzi
Valeri, *Lodovico* 1: p. 651).

41. The triumphal arches may have had
their model in the piazza at Cre-
mona. On 23 September 1454 Francesco Sforza wrote to the "Praesi-
dentes negotiis Cremonae":
"Habiamo inteso della laudabile
deliberatione avete fatta de solare
la piazza e de fare un arco con due
statue in honore et memoria di noi
e della nostra praecordialissima
consorte." The statues were sup-
posed to be made by Filarete, but
the project apparently was not
carried out; see M. Lazzaroni and
A. Muñoz, *Filarete* (Rome, 1908),
p. 181. Nearly contemporary with
the arches of Vigevano and evidently also closely related to them
in form was the "arco trionfale

sopra colonne grandi," erected in front of the high altar in the Cathedral of Milan for the wedding of Maximilian I and Bianca Maria Sforza, which Beatrice, the wife of Il Moro, described in a letter from Vigevano on 28 December 1493 to her sister Isabella d'Este: ". . . era tutto dipinto et haveva nel fronte la effigie del quondam Duca Francesco [Sforza] a cavallo . . . et l'arma del Re de'Romani di sopra. Questo arco trionfale, fatto in quadro, haveva ornamento di pitture fatte di feste antique; et la parte che guardava verso l'altare grande teneva le insigne imperiali nella parte più excelsa [e] sotto l'arma del illustrissimo signor mio consorte" (A. Luzio, "Delle relazioni di Isabella d'Este Gonzaga con Lodovico e Beatrice Sforza," *Archivio Storico Lombardo*, 18 [1890]: pp. 384ff.).

42. Regarding the question of the attribution of the piazza, scholarship has scarcely advanced beyond the positions of Malaguzzi Valeri, *Lodovico* 2: pp. 478ff., for Leonardo's activity in Vigevano; 2: pp. 158ff., 170ff., for Bramante's in, respectively, the castle and the piazza; and of Bruschi, *Bramante*, pp. 647ff. The date of Bramante's presence there given by Bruschi, *ibid.*, pp. 805, 812 should be corrected from 1492 to 13 April 1494; see C. Baroni, *Documenti per la storia dell'architettura a Milano nel rinascimento e nel barocco* (Florence, 1940), 1: p. 46, #1 and documents fol. 37 *verso*, 38. For Giovannoni, ". . . non v'è alcun dubbio nell' attribuzione che essa (piazza) risalga al disegno del Bramante" (*Saggi*, p. 287).

43. See Bruschi, *Bramante*, p. 785. Among them were probably the ten

columns "cum sue base e capitelli" delivered to Bramante, according to a document, on 16 February 1494 (Malaguzzi Valeri, *Lodovico* 2: p. 161).

44. See L. Beltrami, *Bramante a Milano* (Milan, 1912), pp. 12ff., and excerpts in Malaguzzi Valeri, *Lodovico* 2: p. 161. Bramante's activity in Vigevano is also mentioned in Cesariano's 1552 edition of Vitruvius, book VII, chap. 2, p. 113.

45. See Edmondo Solmi, *Scritti Vinciani*, pp. 94, 85. Regarding the paintings recorded by Leonardo (in *Ms. H.*, fol. 129), which Solmi relates to the facade of the piazza (*ibid.*, p. 88), Malaguzzi Valeri says correctly that the record contains no reference to Vigevano and that it could refer to the decoration of an interior since "smalto, azzurro, oro e altri colori" were hardly used for exterior frescoes (*Lodovico* 2: p. 479).

46. Ludovico il Moro calls Ambrogio di Corte "Magister generalis aulae nostrae" and "nostro maestro di casa universale"; see Colombo, "Piazza Ducale," p. 248. In 1493 Ambrogio was also instructed to pay reparations to the owners of the houses destroyed in the building of the piazza "secundo la limitatione e discrecione de esso Ambrosio" (*ibid.*, p. 249).

47. See Bruschi, who sees in the triumphal arches "le parti forse più bramantesche dell' intervento" (*Bramante*, p. 651).

48. The best survey and analysis of the frescoes is found *ibid.*, pp. 111ff.

49. F. Graf Wolff Metternich, "Der Kupferstich Bernardos de Prevedari aus Mailand von 1481," *Römisches*

Jahrbuch für Kunstgeschichte 11 (1967–68): pp. 70ff., 78ff. (with references to Vigevano). On the other hand, see the completely different conception of the basket capital in Francesco di Giorgio Martini, *Trattati di architettura ingegneria e arte militare,* C. Maltese, ed., 2 vols. (Milan, 1967): 2, pl. 220.

50. Malaguzzi Valeri, *Lodovico* 2: p. 157. As has been shown, Bramante was in Vigevano once more in February, 1494. Bramante's indifference to the execution of his designs, which can be inferred from his absence, would correspond exactly to Leonardo's maxim "l'ordinare è opera signorile, l'operare è atto servile" (*Cod. Atl.,* fol. 109 *recto*).

51. Berghoef, "Origines" (pp. 173ff., Figs. 16, 21–22) interprets the Leonardo sketch (*Ms. B.,* fol. 16 *recto*) as a design for the piazza and the reconstruction of the castle in Vigevano. The piazza facade in the sketch is in point of fact closely related to the plan of the piazza in Vigevano, with loggias on the ground floor, round-headed windows on the *piano nobile,* and tondi in the mezzanine above. But the palazzo, which Leonardo places next to the piazza, would be in front of the castle tower, which is not shown in the drawing, and on the site occupied by the ramp between the triple triumphal arch and the entrance to the castle. Thus, in any case the drawing must be dated before the working studies for the piazza. It is, however, unlikely that the old network of streets in Vigevano, which after all was preserved for the most part when the piazza was built, was intended to be changed so radically. Perhaps the sketch depicts an ideal project, in which Vigevano was already the model for Leonardo's piazza facade.

52. For the inscription sealed in when the cornerstone was laid, see Biffignandi, *Memorie,* 1: p. 279. The 1532 wooden model by Antonio da Lonate, now standing in the sacristy of the cathedral, represents a project for the new building; see E. Aschieri, "Il modello ligneo del duomo di Vigevano," *Palladio* 3 (1939): pp. 123ff.

53. See Biffignandi, *Memorie,* 1: p. 333, with a precise and unusually appreciative description of the facade. On the contrary, Barucci says that it is ". . . in istile barocco non elegante nè artistica" (*Castello,* p. 32). See also De Bernardi Ferrero, "Caramuel," pp. 108ff., Figs. 23–30, for the alterations made to the facade in 1910. On Caramuel, see *ibid.,* pp. 91ff., and W. Oechslin, "Osservazioni su Guarino Guarini e Juan Caramuel de Lobkowitz," in *Atti del convegno su Guarino Guarini e l'internazionalità del barocco* (Turin, 1970), pp. 573ff.

54. See Biffignandi, *Memorie,* Barucci, *Castello,* and De Bernardi Ferrero, "Caramuel," passim. It is instructive to note that the reason given for removing the ramp was the annoyance to passers-by, because "giovani di ogni condizioni" used it in the winter for sledding. For the late seventeenth century, the esthetic ideal of the uniform appearance of the piazza was decisive, all the more so because the dynastic relationship symbolized by the association of triumphal arches, ramp, and castle portal had lost its meaning.

55. See Biffignandi, *Memorie,* 1: p. 334, and Colombo, "Armi e leggenda," p. 181. The rents collected from the merchants and the tenants of the

new stores and dwellings went to the episcopal seminary. From this one can conclude that the rents of 1492–94 collected from the old buildings financed by the community were paid to the commune.

56. A uniform coat of paint "a tinta cenerognola con ornato in giallo all' arcate e alle finestre, quasi ad imitare la nuova facciata del Duomo" now replaced the Quattrocento polychrome facade decoration (Colombo, "Piazza Ducale," p. 249). The seventeenth-century paint on the cathedral facade is still intact. In 1757, the piazza facades were whitewashed once more; our Fig. 79 shows the coat of paint applied then, which is mentioned by Colombo (*ibid.*) and was removed by the modern restorer. (Fig. 79 is taken from the lithograph in *Alcuni vedute della città di Vigevano,* Milan, 1846.)

57. On the concept of the "piazza-salone" see Chap. 7; Lotz, "Sansovinos Bibliothek," pp. 336ff.; and Bruschi, *Bramante,* pp. 648ff.

58. The author is indebted to Dipl. Ing. Gert Kaster for expert advice, and to Architect W. Frankl for the drawings illustrated in Figs. C, D, E.

5
THE ROMAN LEGACY IN SANSOVINO'S VENETIAN BUILDINGS

Jacopo Sansovino was forty-one years old when he arrived in Venice in 1527. His great Venetian buildings, the Library of San Marco (Fig. 81) and the Palazzo Cornaro (Fig. 82), were designed in the thirties and forties. It has often been observed that the monumentality and grandeur of Sansovino's Venetian style have no antecedents in Venetian architecture, but little has been done to investigate the sources of the artist's style. Yet fifty-year-old architects of the sixteenth century were usually mature and well-defined artistic personalities.[1] This paper, then, has a twofold purpose. It will try to characterize Sansovino's ambience during his early years in Florence and Rome, emphasizing the structures with which Sansovino is known or can be surmised to have been involved; and it will attempt to trace certain elements of Sansovino's Venetian buildings back to his Roman years.

When the Procuratori di San Marco appointed Sansovino as *proto* (chief architect) of the church in 1529, they recorded that they had "excellent information that Sansovino was sufficiently and well qualified as an architect."[2] The document refers clearly to the repair work the artist had done on the domes of San Marco in 1527 and 1529, but it may also imply that the Procuratori had reports about Sansovino's activity as an architect before his arrival in Venice. Such an activity is indeed mentioned by Vasari, who says that Sansovino designed the Palazzo Gaddi and the Church of San Giovanni dei Fiorentini in Rome and, earlier still, the decorations for the entry of Pope Leo X into Florence.[3] Sansovino's project for San Giovanni dei Fiorentini was never executed; the Florentine decorations of 1515, done in plaster and wood, were of a temporary kind. Thus the Palazzo Gaddi appears to be the only extant structure from Vasari's catalogue. But this palace is a relatively modest edifice; it offers little that can be compared with the much more grandiose enterprises of Sansovino's Venetian years.

There is no reason to doubt Vasari's statement that Jacopo started his

Published in the *Journal of the Society of Architectural Historians* 22 (1963): pp. 3–12 career as an apprentice in Andrea Sansovino's workshop. Andrea was in Rome from 1505 to 1512; his tombs of the nephews of Pope Julius II stand in the choir of Santa Maria del Popolo, which was designed by Bramante. Before he went to Rome, Andrea had worked with Giuliano da Sangallo in the sacristy of Santo Spirito in Florence.[4] The names of Andrea Sansovino and Bramante occur in the documents for the Santa Casa of Loreto, one of the Pope's favorite projects.[5]

Vasari tells us that Jacopo Sansovino was brought to Rome and introduced to the Pope by Giuliano da Sangallo and that Bramante asked the young sculptor to make a copy of the Laocoön.[6] Whether or not this is literally true, it certainly indicates that Jacopo Sansovino, then in his twenties, was familiar with the great building enterprises of Julius II and his friends, such as the new St. Peter's or the Farnesina. The papal architect, Bramante, was then in his early sixties; he was about ten years older than Andrea Sansovino and Giuliano da Sangallo.

From 1512 to 1518, Jacopo was back in Florence, working mostly as a sculptor. During this period he contributed to the decorations for the triumphal entry of Leo X into Florence. According to Vasari—again our only source—Jacopo designed the wooden facade to cover the incomplete Trecento front of Santa Maria del Fiore during the celebrations. The sham facade was, in Vasari's words, "of the Corinthian order . . . in the shape of a triumphal arch; Sansovino had placed double columns on very high bases, and there were certain niches containing statues in the round; higher up there were large-sized reliefs, of bronzelike color; above there followed architraves, friezes and cornices, and also various beautiful pediments."[7]

Vasari goes on to say that the Pope was so impressed by Sansovino's sham facade that Leo asked him for a project for the facade of San Lorenzo and that Baccio d'Agnolo made a wooden model after Sansovino's design. For this commission Jacopo had to compete with Raphael and Michelangelo. Presumably all three artists were familiar with the projects Giuliano da Sangallo had submitted for San Lorenzo shortly before his death in 1516.

We have already seen that Sangallo had worked with Jacopo's foster father on Santo Spirito in Florence and that Vasari mentions him as the young Jacopo's protector in Rome. Thus there can be little doubt that Giuliano and Jacopo were on rather close terms. There also seems to be visual evidence for their relation. Giuliano's drawings for San Lorenzo, now in the Uffizi, include a rather puzzling sheet that comes from Vasari's collection (Fig. 83). It has several inscriptions from Giuliano's hand: his own signature appears, rather oddly placed, upside-down on top of the drawing; over the three portals one reads "storie di S. Lorenzo." At first sight, then, the sheet appears to be a project made for the facade of the Florentine church. Yet this is not the whole story.[8] The facade has two shields for coats of arms, a blank one in the crowning pediment and a smaller one over one of the statues of the main order. In the latter, one can recognize the della Rovere arms. Moreover, the statuary and especially the reliefs in the attic do not indicate a church dedicated to the martyr. *The Adoration of the Child* over the main portal has as little to do with St. Lawrence as the Annunciation shown under the lateral gables. All this can best be explained if we assume that the artist adapted a drawing made for another occasion for the new commission of San Lorenzo. It is unthinkable that he ever suggested the shield of Julius II for the family church of the Medici in Florence. Rather, the evidence points to a facade planned by the della Rovere Pope for a church dedicated to the Virgin. In our context it can only be suggested that the drawing was in all probability originally a project for the facade of the Church of the Santa Casa in Loreto, the dome of which Giuliano da Sangallo had vaulted in 1500.[9] At any rate, this sheet was drawn during the pontificate of Julius II. If one accepts this, one can also suppose that this or similar drawings were known to Jacopo Sansovino when he prepared his decorations of Santa Maria del Fiore in 1515. As a matter of fact, Vasari's description of Jacopo's wooden facade could be used equally for Giuliano's drawing.[10]

Now the motif of the double columns which one sees here in Giuliano's version appears at least twice in Bramante's oeuvre. In the Palazzo Caprini, Bramante used engaged double columns of the Doric order to articulate the *piano nobile*. More important for our context is the second example, the decoration of the Santa Casa in Loreto (Fig. 84), where one finds Corinthian double columns and niches with statues, that is, the same arrangement which we saw in Giuliano's drawings and which Sansovino used in his wooden facade of 1515.

One of the first actions of Leo X after his election in 1513 was to appoint Andrea Sansovino chief architect of the Church of the Santa Casa, an office formerly held by Bramante.[11] Andrea was of course also responsible for the decoration of the Santa Casa, the architectural framework of which Bramante had designed. We have seen that Giuliano da Sangallo had also worked in Loreto; it is not farfetched to assume that he too was familiar with Bramante's design for the Santa Casa.

Thus the pattern of Bramante's Santa Casa appears to be the ultimate source of Giuliano da Sangallo's as well as of Jacopo Sansovino's facade with their double columns arranged "sopra un grande imbasamento," as Vasari puts it. And the motif was to become a standard feature of Jacopo's Venetian facades. It occurs as late as 1557 in his front of San Geminiano, the church demolished under Napoleon (Fig. 85); and we find it, in a fashion derived from the Palazzo Caprini, in the upper stories of the Palazzo Cornaro. Also he planned to use it for the unfinished front of the Scuola Grande della Misericordia. The drawing for the latter facade in Vicenza, usually ascribed to Palladio (Fig. 86), may very well be a rendering of Sansovino's project, and here again Vasari's words about Jacopo's wooden decoration of Santa Maria del Fiore could be applicable.[12]

Finally, the motif appears in Sansovino's Loggietta, in which four pairs of columns flank three roundheaded portals of equal height and width (Fig. 87). This arrangement cannot be derived directly from the Roman triumphal arches, which do not have three openings of the same size or paired columns. But the rhythmical grouping of columns in the Loggia is once more almost identical with the main order of Giuliano da Sangallo's project, although in such details as the separate bases of the columns and the breaking of the entablature Sansovino does hark back to the Roman arches.

Let us now turn to Sansovino's second sojourn in Rome. It lasted from 1518 to 1527, except for the years from 1521 to 1523, when he was in Florence and possibly in Venice. Soon after his arrival in Rome he obtained the commission for San Giovanni dei Fiorentini. According to Vasari, Leo X decided in favor of Sansovino's project for the church, against those submitted by Raphael, Antonio da Sangallo the Younger, and Peruzzi.[13] The story is corroborated by a letter written in 1537 by Pietro Aretino. In our context it may be worth mentioning that Sansovino competed here with the major architects working during the reign of Leo X, all men in their thirties. This alone seems to prove that Sansovino at that time was no longer considered to be a beginner; his project must have been recognized as a conspicuous achievement.

San Giovanni is actually Jacopo's first architectural job for which there is documentary proof. On 7 January 1520, he was paid for services there, which involved a model. Another entry in the records, dated 30 January, mentions that Antonio da Sangallo also had made a model.[14] It is difficult to decide whether the two entries refer to the same or to two different objects. Sansovino's design, which won so much praise, unfortunately is lost, and Vasari's description is too general to allow a reconstruction. The building campaign, which began in 1520 apparently under Jacopo's direction, was frustrated by insuperable difficulties encountered with the foundations. Since in 1520 both Sangallo and Sansovino were paid as architects of the church, it must be assumed that they worked as a team and that Jacopo knew of and approved what his colleague did. Of course, this would apply as well to the drawings Sangallo submitted during this period to the *operai*. I would like to concentrate on a single feature which recurs in the whole series of Antonio's studies for San Giovanni: namely, the shape of the pier suggested for the nave of the church.

In his drawing (Fig. 88), a rapid sketch, Sangallo superimposes three different schemes for the ground plan.[15] One recognizes: a centralizing plan with square chapels around a circular space; a longitudinal plan with a nave of three bays; and a longitudinal plan with a nave of five bays. The facade for all schemes is the same, and they all show the same type of square pier with an engaged column. At the time this sheet was made, it was obviously still undecided whether the church would have a centralizing or a longitudinal plan—yet the sketch shows the same pier in all three renderings. Therefore, it seems safe to conclude that this drawing stems from an early stage in the planning process and that the shape of the pier as shown was agreed upon from the beginning of Sangallo's activity for San Giovanni. In other words, if Sansovino was Sangallo's teammate in the earliest phase of the building campaign, then he must have known the shape of the piers suggested by Sangallo, and his own project may well have provided for the same kind of pier. It should be stressed that this particular pier occurs in all of Sangallo's drawings for San Giovanni, whether the suggested scheme is centralizing or longitudinal.

This pier was by no means commonly used during the early Cinquecento. It derives, of course, from such ancient structures as the Theater of Marcellus, and it occurs in the Albertian courtyard of the Palazzo Venezia. But Bramante did not employ it in St. Peter's and in his other churches, and his piers in the Cortile del Belvedere and in the cloister of Santa Maria della Pace have engaged pilasters. However, the pier is found in an unexecuted building designed by Bramante, the court of the Palazzo di Giustizia in the Via Giulia.[16]

On the other hand, the motif does occur in the most conspicuous court-yard that was under construction during Sansovino's second Roman sojourn, in the Palazzo Farnese (Fig. 89).[17] The earliest arcades of this court stem from a building campaign begun in 1517. They are almost contemporary with the projects for San Giovanni dei Fiorentini, where the same pier is used by the same architect, Antonio da Sangallo the Younger. It can be taken for granted that Sansovino was familiar with the new palace. San Giovanni dei Fiorentini and the Palazzo Farnese are linked by the Via Giulia, the same street, incidentally, where one still can see the lower story of Bramante's Palazzo di Giustizia, the court of which was to have the very same type of pier.

This particular pier with the engaged column also is used in Sansovino's Library of San Marco, begun in 1537. While the sculptural decoration of Sansovino's building is richer than anything found in Rome, the architec-tural profiles correspond rather closely to those of the Farnese court as it appears in an elevation depicting the court as planned by Sangallo, that is, before its later alterations (Fig. 90). Over the earliest arcades of the Farnese court there are still some of the original, disklike metopes of 1517, and an almost identical design is to be observed in the metopes which adorn the frieze of the Doric order of the Library.

There is another building of the second decade of the Cinquecento that offers an even closer analogy to the architectural vocabulary of Sansovino's Library, the church of Santa Maria presso San Biagio in·Montepulciano (Fig. 91). San Biagio was begun in 1518; the architect was the brother of Giuliano and the uncle of Antonio da Sangallo the Younger.[18] Montepul-ciano is only a few miles from Monte San Savino, and it lies on one of the old routes that connect Rome and Florence. Thus it is highly probable that Jacopo Sansovino knew the church.

In the interior of San Biagio the corner piers consist of an engaged column and a pilaster. The triglyphs of the Doric frieze are placed over the column and the pilaster respectively, and a disk is inserted over the gap between the two vertical members. The same arrangement may be seen in the famous corner pier of the Library. The similarity seems too close to be accidental, especially since Sansovino's trips to and from Rome coincided with the building dates of Montepulciano. It is tempting to assume not only that Jacopo was familiar with San Biagio but also that he made or obtained drawings of the interior of the church, which he later used for the Library.

Incidentally, the same compound corner pier appears as well in Sangallo's project for San Giovanni dei Fiorentini, which has been discussed
already with respect to the piers with the engaged columns (Fig. 88). The
drawing shows only a rapid sketch of the facade, yet it is clear that the
draftsman planned to have a corner pier of the shape that Sansovino chose
for the Library.

The Doric and Ionic orders of the Library with their rich articulation
and ornamentation have justly been admired. I do not propose to discuss
here the old problem of the priority of the so-called "Serliana," for Serlio's
fourth book, published in 1537, shows the motif in almost the identical
fashion as it appears in the upper story of the Library, the construction of
which was begun in the same year. Both Sansovino and Serlio certainly had
seen Bramante's window in what is now the Sala Regia of the Vatican:[19] a
tripartite opening where a slightly wider, roundheaded central bay is
flanked by trabeated lateral bays. The round arch sits over columns; the
flanking bays have pilasters. In Serlio's illustration and in the Library this
motif is incorporated in a major system of engaged columns. By this device
the width of the opening proper could be narrowed and the thickness of
the structural walls increased without making the front walls appear too
heavy.

Sansovino had to deal with a specific structural problem. The Ionic order
of the Library partakes of the buttressing system the architect had to provide in order to balance the thrust of the great barrel vault he planned for
the upper story of the building.[20] It was advisable to strengthen the outer
walls, which had to support the barrel vault. Sansovino's "Serliana" offers
a highly original and satisfactory solution for this structural requirement.

In this context one may look back once more to the projects for San
Giovanni dei Fiorentini of 1520 and to Sangallo's drawing in particular,
which shows the engaged column as it appears later in the Doric order of
the Library (Fig. 88). In the clerestory Sangallo did not intend to open up
the full width of the wall between the engaged columns; rather, he has the
columns framing the aedicula, which in turn frames a roundheaded window. Thus a minor system of engaged columns is enframed by the higher
and thicker columns of a major system. To be sure, the smaller columns do
not support the arch of the opening proper as they do in the Library. Yet
the resulting narrowing of the window may well be compared with the
"Serliana" of the Library, the more so because the structural function of
Sangallo's arrangement—namely, to increase the stability of the weight-

supporting walls—resembles the function of Sansovino's system. Sangallo could not have wished to endanger the coherence of the clerestory walls by making the windows too large. Ingenious and entirely novel though it is, the "Serliana" of Sansovino's Library may be seen as the fusion of the tripartite window, which he knew from Bramante's Sala Regia, and the combination of a major and a minor system suggested by Sangallo for San Giovanni.

The pier with the engaged column appears once more in Sansovino's oeuvre, namely in the Villa Garzoni at Ponte Casale, usually dated to the 1540s (Fig. 92).[21] The two-storied loggia of the facade is derived clearly from the Farnese court as it was planned when Sansovino was in Rome. The resemblance is even closer here than in the Library, for the Villa Garzoni has no "Serliana," and the rich sculptural decoration of the Library is missing. The motif of the pier with the engaged column recurs in the courtyard of the Villa. Although executed in brick and devoid of all decoration, the Doric order of the court again harks back to that of the Roman palace. Sangallo's drawing (Fig. 90), depicting the Farnese court as it was planned originally, and Sansovino's loggia at Ponte Casale are almost identical in the design of the Doric and Ionic orders. It should be pointed out that at the time Sansovino left Rome the courtyard of the new Farnese Palace resembled the Theater of Marcellus more than any other Roman loggia then extant or under construction.

The pier with the engaged column, then, appears to be just as characteristic a feature of Sansovino's Venetian structures as the double column he used in his facades and in the Loggietta. It does not seem purely accidental that the two leitmotifs Sansovino retained from the architectural repertory of his Roman ambience are both markedly three-dimensional in nature. The engaged column enhances the volume of a pier, the double column emphasizes the relief of a facade. For Sansovino a facade was primarily a sequence of three-dimensional members—piers, columns, entablatures, and so forth—and not a two-dimensional plane. In this respect Sansovino's structures have more in common with ancient architecture than with the buildings erected by Sangallo, Peruzzi, or Giulio Romano in the 1530s and 1540s. It was the forceful plasticity, the implied emotions of strength and dignity, that made the double column and the pier with the engaged column so attractive to Jacopo. In this sense one may see him as the real heir of Bramante, whose Tempietto embodies all of these qualities to such a high degree. In fact, both motifs discussed could well have been derived from Bramante. Perhaps Vasari had this in mind when he wrote about the Library: "This edifice was the reason why the Venetians began to build with new designs and in better order and according to the ancient discipline of Vitruvius. This is true both for public and private building. In the judgment of the experts and of those who have seen a good deal of the world, this building has no peer."[22]

There is still another feature of the Library which appears to be a reminiscence of Jacopo's Roman years. The entablature of the Ionic order has a frieze of garland-carrying putti. In the middle of each bay the garlands are attached to a small oval window (Fig. 93). A very similar frieze of putti and garlands adorns the attic of the Farnesina (Fig. 94). Here, too, it serves to incorporate or to conceal, as it were, the windows of the upper mezzanine. The frieze of the Farnesina was paid for in 1521, that is, during Sansovino's Roman period,[23] and there seems to be no reason to doubt that he was familiar with the building, which faces the Farnese palace on the other side of the Tiber River. Of course, Sansovino's windows are stylistically more advanced than the square openings of the Farnesina, his garlands richer and heavier, yet the similarity of form and function seems too close to be accidental.[24]

At first glance the frieze of the Library appears as a merely decorative detail. But it demonstrates beautifully the unique integration of sculpture and architecture that is perhaps the most striking trait of the building. Sansovino placed his putti over the engaged columns of the piers, accentuating and reiterating thereby the verticality of the columns in the horizontal band of the frieze. This is noticeable even from a relatively distant point of view, although the beholder may not be consciously aware of it. In the Farnesina frieze, on the other hand, oddly-shaped ornamental contraptions are set over the pilasters, to which the garlands are affixed. They are so inconspicuous that they do not interrupt the horizontal rhythm of putti and garlands. The frieze gives the impression of a decorative addition to the structural system of the two main stories. But in the library the anthropomorphous elements of the frieze become an indispensable member of the structural organism—indispensable because they effect the transition from the weighty, engaged columns to the statues crowning the attic. This may be seen best at the corner piers towards San Marco. Reading from the ground floor upwards, one sees the columns next to the pilasters in both stories. In the frieze the putto is over the column, and the garland he holds hangs from a lion's head placed at the corner pier and therefore equally visible from both sides. The statue of the attic reiterates the verticality of the columns and the putto. Next to the statue the much higher obelisk, just like the lion's head below, offers the same aspect to the two sides. Thus Sansovino has transformed the purely ornamental motif of the Farnesina into a highly effective member of his system, a system whose novelty and beauty lie in the consonance of sculptural-anthropomorphous and structural-architectural elements.

Notes

1. For the bibliography on Sansovino see U. Thieme and F. Becker, *Lexikon* 32: pp. 465ff; and Venturi, *Storia* 11/3: pp. 100ff.

2. The *procuratori* declared themselves "optime informati de sufficientia et bonitate Jacopi Sansovini Architecti." The often-printed document of 7 April 1529 is found in L. Pittoni, *Jacopo Sansovino Scultore* (Venice, 1909), p. 151 (hereafter, Pittoni, *Sansovino*).

3. See Vasari, *Opere*, G. Milanesi, ed. 7: 494ff. Another description of the wooden facade is in L. Landucci, *Diario Fiorentino dal 1450 al 1516*, J. Del Badia, ed. (Florence, 1883), p. 356—" . . . aveva alla facciata 12 colonne di marmo alte e maggiori che quelle di San Lorenzo, co' magni archi trionfali alle porte."

4. For a discussion of Andrea Sansovino's work in Santo Spirito, see U. Middeldorf, "Giuliano da Sangallo and Andrea Sansovino," *Art Bulletin* 16 (1934): pp. 107ff; and G.H. Huntley, *Sansovino*, pp. 83ff.

5. See Huntley, *Sansovino*, pp. 88ff.; and Giovannoni, *Saggi*, p. 97.

6. See Vasari, *Opere* 7: p. 489.

7. See *ibid.*, p. 494.

8. A catalogue of Sangallo's projects for San Lorenzo is found in Marchini, *Sangallo*, pp. 100ff; see also R. Pommer, "Drawings for the Facade of San Lorenzo by Guiliano da Sangallo," (M. A. thesis, Institute of Fine Arts, New York University, 1957).

9. Marchini, *Sangallo*, p. 100.

10. See p. 141 for a translation of Vasari's text.

11. See Huntley, *Sansovino*, p. 114.

12. For the drawing see R. Pane, *Andrea Palladio* (Turin, 1961), p. 312 and Fig. 78.

13. The complicated building history of this church was discussed in H. Siebenhüner, "S. Giovanni dei Fiorentini in Rom," *Kunstgeschichtliche Studien für Hans Kauffmann* (Berlin, 1956), pp. 172ff. (hereafter, Siebenhüner, "S. Giovanni") and in Giovannoni, *Sangallo*, 1: pp. 214ff. I find myself unable to accept Siebenhüner's attempt to attribute Uffizi A 1312 to Sansovino and to identify it with his project for San Giovanni.

14. 7 January, 1520—"maestro Jachopo Sansovino alias loro architectore . . . tanto per conto di suo servizio quanto di modello"; 30 January—"Antonio da Sangallo loro architectore non era anchora stato

satisfacto [paid] d'uno modello della chiesa avante fatto" (see— with the full entries—A. Nava, "La storia della Chiesa di S. Giovanni dei Fiorentini nei documenti del suo archivio," *Archivio della R. Deputazione Romana di Storia Patria* 59 [1936]: pp. 340ff.). Contrary to Siebenhüner, "S. Giovanni," p. 185, the word *alias* in the entry about Sansovino seems to indicate that Sansovino was still the architect of the church in January, 1520.

15. Besides the discussion of the drawing in Siebenhüner and Giovannoni (see note 13), see the brilliant analysis by Ackerman, "Architectural Practice," p. 9.

16. The ground plan of Bramante's project for the palace is only preserved in drawings by his followers, such as Sangallo's sheet in the Uffizi, reproduced in Venturi, *Storia* 11/1: p. 116, and C. Baroni, *Bramante* (Bergamo, n.d. [1944]), p.113 (hereafter, Baroni, *Bramante*).

17. See Giovannoni, *Sangallo*, 1: pp. 150ff. and Ackerman, *Michelangelo* 2: pp. 67ff.

18. See "Notizie relative al Tempio di San Biagio in Montepulciano," *Bollettino del Centro di Studi di Storia dell'Architecttura* 6 (1952): p. 45.

19. An illustration of the window is found in Baroni, *Bramante*, p. 120.

20. It should be remembered that the vault constructed by Sangallo over the second story of the Library collapsed on 18 December 1545. During the subsequent investigation Sansovino, who had been jailed after the mishap, explained to the *procuratori* that ". . . il volto era largo piedi 32 [about 11 m.]." When asked, "quando vui fusti per refar questa fabrica la refaresti in volto opur in traedura?", he answered, "La saria più sicura et de mancho periculo a farla in travadura" (see Pittoni, *Sansovino,* pp. 170ff.).

21. The Roman character of the loggia of the Villa Garzoni was recognized by G. Lorenzetti in his edition of Vasari's *Vita di Jacopo Tatti detto il Sansovino* (Florence, 1913), p. 43; see also A. Callegari, "Il Palazzo Garzoni a Ponte Casale," *Dedalo* 6 (1926): pp. 569ff.

22. Vasari, *Opere* 7: p. 503.

23. The building accounts for the Farnesina contain the following entry for 1521—"per fare la forma del freso [fregio] che gira dentorno al palazzo." E. Gerlini interpreted this as referring to work done shortly before the entry was made (*La Villa Farnesina in Roma* [Rome, 1949], p. 9); C. L. Frommel would prefer an earlier date for the frieze and understands the entry as part of a summary listing all work done (*Die Farnesina und Peruzzis Architektonisches Frühwerk* [Berlin, 1961], p. 31).

24. This does not contradict Lorenzetti's observation that Sansovino's frieze of the Library may have been inspired by the two garland-holding putti from the fragment of a Roman sarcophagus now in the Museo Archeologico, Venice (*Venezia e il suo Estuario* [Venice, 1926], pp. 691, 696). It should be pointed out that a comparable frieze occurs also in the courtyard of the Palazzo Gaddi Niccolini in Rome, attributed by Vasari to Sansovino; see P. Letarouilly, *Les Edifices de Rome Moderne* (Paris, 1868), 2: pl. 15.

Postscript

Deborah Howard has noted that I had incorrectly stated that the west side of the Piazzetta had no arcade when Sansovino arrived in Venice. "Evidence to the contrary is provided by M. A. Sabellico, Del Sito di Venezia Città (1502), G. Meneghetti ed. (Venice, 1957)" (*Jacopo Sansovino, Architecture and Patronage in Renaissance Venice* (New Haven and London, 1975), p. 161, note 15, and pp. 101ff.). Miss Howard's book has a selected bibliography on Sansovino's Venetian architecture and the Piazza San Marco (pp. 187ff.). See also Manfredo Tafuri, *Jacopo Sansovino e l'architettura del '500 a Venezia* (Padua, 1969).

6
ITALIAN ARCHITECTURE IN THE LATER
SIXTEENTH CENTURY

Seven decades have passed since the publication of Heinrich Wölfflin's *Renaissance and Baroque,* the first attempt to define the styles of sixteenth-century architecture in Italy. Wölfflin's unique combination of felicitous generalization and acute analysis makes his book still indispensable for the student of the period; moreover, his is one of those few art-historical treatises that are understood and appreciated by the unspecialized reader. Impressive though Wölfflin's definitions were, however, they turned out to be too broad to do justice to the complexity of the Cinquecento. They were first enriched and then replaced by a maze of subsidiary and more refined terms, such as Late Renaissance, Proto- and Early Baroque, Classicism, Early-, High-, and Late Mannerism. To illustrate the puzzling situation that confronts us, in 1935 the *Art Bulletin* carried an article entitled "The First Baroque Church in Rome"; this same church, the Gesù, appears later as a Mannerist building in Nikolaus Pevsner's *Outline of European Architecture,* published in 1943. Surely the question, "What is the style of the Gesù?" is a legitimate one. Let us try to answer it by briefly surveying some buildings planned during the 1550s and 1560s, just before the cornerstone of the Gesù was laid in 1568.

Dupérac's well-known engravings of Michelangelo's project for the Capitoline area are dated 1568 and 1569 (Fig. 61). Published after Michelangelo's death, they demonstrate both the impression this project made upon his contemporaries and the belief that the plan should and would be realized to the letter. One should recall Vasari's report that Piero Ligorio was dismissed from the *fabbrica* of St. Peter's in 1565 because he had tried to change Michelangelo's design. Both Vasari and Dupérac must have felt that there was no chance of improving or, as we would say, modernizing Michelangelo's ideas. His projects were declared inviolable; an artist living after Il Divino could only be an epigone. This feeling of an overwhelming past and a feeble present permeates, it seems to me, not only

Published in the *College Art Journal* 17, no. 2 (1958): pp. 129–139

Vasari's *Lives,* but also Giacomo da Vignola's *Cinque Ordini di Architettura,* published in 1562, and Andrea Palladio's treatise on architecture, published in 1570. The ideals prevailing in the 1550s and 1560s were regularity, symmetry, orderliness, and the correct use of rules laid down in ancient architecture or by the "divine" modern masters.

In this context it is revealing that Serlio's treatise on architecture, written in the second quarter of the century, discusses and illustrates many contemporary works, such as Saint Peter's, the Villa Madama, and the Cortile del Belvedere. Palladio, on the other hand, deals aside from his own buildings and the ancient monuments, only with Bramante's Tempietto, which was the most classical of all modern structures. Palladio's interest in Bramante is also proved by his drawing of Bramante's Palazzo Caprini in Rome. As Rudolf Wittkower has pointed out, the derivation of Palladio's facade of the Palazzo Porto Colleoni in Vicenza from Bramante's palace "is too obvious to need any comment." Here were the equilibrium and regularity that Palladio was looking for; he had no use for the disquieting, tense, and nonconformist style developed during the 1530s and 1540s by such Raphaelites as Giulio Romano in Mantua and Peruzzi in Rome.

Another instance of the craving for classical balance, so characteristic in the middle of the century, is furnished by Michele Sanmicheli's later works in Verona. A comparison of his Palazzo Bevilacqua, built about 1530, and the Palazzo Pompei, dated 1555 (Figs. 95 and 96), shows clearly enough the complex and involved application of the orders in the earlier facade as opposed to the quiet regularity of the later structure. This is not a contrast of ancient and modern forms, but one of quiet and agitated interpretations of the antique. The outstanding example of an orthodox and somewhat rigid application of the ancient orders is Palladio's facade of the Palazzo Chiericati in Vicenza, built between 1551 and 1554. As Wittkower stressed, the Doric here "has still something of the simple grandeur of Bramante's Tempietto."

This rational and purist interpretation of antiquity was by no means restricted to Verona and Vicenza. It may also be seen in a project for Santa Maria presso San Celso in Milan (Fig. 97), which can be attributed to Cristoforo Lombardo and which is closely related to his projects for the Certosa in Pavia. The idea of a two-storied, columnated portico in front of the church proper seems to have no analogy in sixteenth-century architecture, but it appears as a logical step in the long series of attempts to reconcile the ancient temple front with the facade of the Christian church.

Vignola's treatise of 1562 is perhaps the most outspoken pronouncement of the new orthodoxy. Trained as a painter, Vignola had worked in France during the early 1540s, together with Serlio, Primaticcio, and Niccolo dell' Abbate. All these artists came from Bologna, and their work in Fontainebleau continued, in many respects, the style developed by Giulio Romano in Mantua. After his return to Italy, Vignola designed the Palazzo Bocchi in Bologna. An engraving of 1555 seems to render Vignola's original project of about 1545 (Fig. 98). With its wildly rusticated blocks, its obelisks, its rich sculptural decoration, this design shows clearly enough the point of departure of Vignola's style, namely the artistic entourage of Francis I at Fontainebleau.

A few years later Vignola provided the design for the Casino of the Villa of Pope Julius III in Rome. The relation of its facade to the Palazzo Bocchi project is obvious. John Coolidge remarks, however, that both the window frames and the portal of the Casino are "duller than those Vignola had himself designed for the Palazzo Bocchi" and that Vignola, unlike Giulio Romano who invented this type of frame, "deliberately avoids a suggestion of struggle; the effect is one of balance, of well-bred compromise."

The process of toning down is carried further in Vignola's facades of Caprarola, begun in 1559. There the wall appears completely flattened; the system of pilasters recalls the tranquil facades of the Farnesina rather than the involved relation of receding and protruding elements of the Villa Giulia.

Thus we find, both in Northern Italy and in Rome during the 1550s and 1560s, a striving for composure, for regularity, for an orthodox use of the ancient orders. Such conformity goes hand in hand with the respect paid to Michelangelo's plans after his death. It is, however, in marked contrast to the fondness for emotional implications, for tension and conflict, found in so many buildings of the second quarter of the century. Even an architect such as Vignola, who by background and training was deeply rooted in the nonconformist tradition of Giulo Romano, conformed to and arrived at a "well-bred compromise."

A comparable process of quieting down may be observed in Michelangelo's later works. His palaces on the Capitol, with all their novel features, bear witness to a much stricter application of the ancient orders than, say, the Laurentian Library, debatable though the comparison of a facade and an interior may be. As early as 1853 Jakob Burckhardt, in his *Cicerone,* called the Library "the first building where the architect purposely defies the meaning of the orders"; confronted with the Capitoline palaces, however, Burckhardt felt "amply compensated for the Laurentian staircase."

Dupérac's engravings show the Capitol as an area, not just as a group of buildings (Fig. 61). The three structures around the equestrian statue of Marcus Aurelius enclose the piazza as if it were the interior of an oblong hall. The attention of the beholder who has walked up the Cordonata, the stairs leading to the piazza, is attracted towards the statue rather than directed towards the Palazzo Senatorio in the rear; furthermore, the beholder is guided away from, and back again to, the statue by the unique pattern of the pavement.

The lack of a specific orientation, the interest in shaping an area rather than isolated buildings, the enclosed character of this area which excludes one from its center: all this seems to point to another important feature of the 1550s and 1560s—the fondness for static space enclosed by walls that do not impart a directional impulse. The very fact that there was, as far as we know, no practical need for the palace on the left (Fig. 61), seems to prove that Michelangelo wanted this building mainly for visual purposes; it was to serve as a facade to enclose the piazza. After its erection, in the seventeenth century, the building got the somewhat meaningless name of Palazzo Nuovo; additional evidence shows that it did not meet an actual requirement.

Another example of such an enclosed area is the courtyard of the Palazzo Pitti, built by Bartolommeo Ammannati in the late 1550's in Florence (Fig. 99). In the Florentine palaces of the fifteenth century, high and wide loggias surrounded the open center of the courtyard. They invited the visitor, by their spaciousness, to stay under their vaults rather than in the center; in the Pitti, the relation of arcades and center is reversed. One can only understand the rustication and articulation of the walls if one stands in the central area or walks along its walls.

Another aspect of this desire for static space is the puzzling re-emergence of the central church about 1550. Needless to say, freestanding central structures encourage the spectator to circulate both around the church and within its walls; this movement is as endless as that around the equestrian statue on the Capitol. Palladio's interest in Bramante's Tempietto was certainly enhanced by this very quality of the structure. Shortly before his death in 1559, Sanmicheli provided the design for Santa Maria di Campagna near Verona, a circular church surrounded by a loggia (Fig. 36). In 1552 Alessi began Santa Maria di Carignano in Genoa, a fully centralized and freestanding church over a square ground plan (Fig. 100). A less familiar example of the square type is Galasso Alghisi's Santa Maria delle Vergini near Macerata, also started in the 1550s. Alessandro Pagliarino, a Milanese architect, drew the plan and the section of this church around 1580 (Figs. 101 and 102).

The re-emergence of the central church is unthinkable without Michelangelo's project for St. Peter's. The well-known fresco in the Vatican Library, although painted after 1580, represents what today would be called an artist's rendering of the plan developed by Michelangelo shortly before 1550 (Fig. 103). It is revealing that the fresco shows a piazza around the church and that this piazza is enclosed on three sides by identical structures. There is no special emphasis on the facade; the semicircular dome hovers above it, but does not seem to surge upwards. In other words, the area around the building, the interior of the church, and even its vault, are equally static, equally lacking direction.

Another fresco, painted only a few years later, shows Michelangelo's facade with the obelisk set up in front of it in 1586 (Fig. 104). At this time the nave of the old St. Peter's was still standing. This fresco, therefore, also represents an artist's rendering rather than a view of what actually existed. The steps leading up to the front of the church already appear in the earlier fresco, but in the later one they are arranged to indicate a specific direction; they are seen behind the obelisk and in conjunction with it. The central part of the facade is now framed, as it were, by the statues of St. Peter and St. Paul. There is a crescendo of forms from the obelisk to the facade and its pediment; and then over the small domes to the major dome. This effect is visible on only one side of the church and distinguishes this facade of the building as its front.

Both the site chosen for the obelisk by Pope Sixtus V and the fresco painted about 1590 embody the new concept of oriented, as opposed to static, space; a concept that Maderno was to develop in his later re-interpretation of Michelangelo's central building.

During the plague of 1576, the city of Venice had vowed to build a church in honor of the Redeemer. The committee in charge of the new building decided in favor of a longitudinal plan, pointing out that the scheme of the Gesù in Rome was more satisfactory than the central type. The architect, Palladio, accordingly was instructed to provide a longitudinal plan for the Church of the Redentore. One knows from the building accounts that the Gesù, begun in 1568 by Vignola, was still under construction in 1576; only the nave was complete. Yet the Venetian committee must have realized the significance of Vignola's nave, as indeed have most subsequent critics. A seemingly unimportant feature of the nave may clarify its novelty. Under the main entablature and over the nave arcade there are small balconies or *coretti* that give on to a gallery over the side chapels (Fig. 105). Closed off by wooden screens, from the nave the *coretti* appear as part of the wall surface rather than as openings. The insertion of the gallery makes the chapels lower and darker. The unbroken main entablature, the light coming from the dome, and the width of the apse, all draw the spectator's attention away from the side chapels and toward the crossing area. Indeed, the nave itself, enclosed by relatively unbroken flat walls and the enormous barrel vault, may also be seen as an independent spatial unit. The unbroken entablature carried by double pilasters is a unique feature; the effect is one of equipoise, of quiet monumentality, of static space.

As Rudolf Wittkower has pointed out, the interior of Palladio's Redentore represents a synthesis of the older central and the new, longitudinal or oriented scheme. It would appear that Vignola's Gesù shows precisely the same synthesis in its combination of a wide and, as it were, self-sufficient nave with a domed crossing.

The Milanese church of the Jesuit order, San Fedele, built by Pellegrino Tibaldi, dates from the same decade as the nave of the Gesù. A view of 1622 (Fig. 106) shows the church before its enlargement in the late seventeenth century. The interior consisted originally of two enormous groin-vaulted bays and an apse. As in the Basilica of Maxentius and the Baths of Diocletian, the vaults are supported by huge, freestanding columns. Thus Tibaldi borrowed structural devices from ancient architecture to create a purely static space, whereas Vignola's church with its entirely novel wall system, which seems to have no analogy in ancient architecture, appears as a synthesis of static and oriented space.

Tibaldi's interior is, of course, unthinkable without Michelangelo's Church of Santa Maria degli Angeli in the Baths of Diocletian. Interestingly enough, Michelangelo's interior may also be described as a juxtaposition of static and directed space. The visitor who enters the portal from the Piazza dell'Esedra is clearly directed towards the main altar; but when he reaches the enormous hall of the former *tepidarium,* that directional impulse is checked by the static space of this "transept."

After 1580 the new concept of oriented space and of spatial crescendo leading towards a visual climax definitely prevailed, both in ecclesiastical and secular architecture, as has been seen in the setting up of the obelisk in front of St. Peter's, and its consequences for the way in which the facade and the dome of the church are perceived. The same stylistic development is particularly striking in garden planning. A comparison of Tribolo's Villa at Castello (about 1550) and Buontalenti's Villa at Pratolino (about 1590), both built for the Medici dukes of Florence, demonstrates the static arrangement of the former and the axial organization of the latter (Figs. 107 and 108). At Castello, walls serve to enclose and articulate gardens; the visitor is invited to circulate around the fountains. In Pratolino, the building sits on top of the hill; the visitor is led up to the *point de vue* on a broad avenue that starts from an oval pond, and the very shape of this pond is determined by the orientation of the whole complex.

Let us come back to the problem of definitions. How should we designate the style of the 1550s? How can the latter be set off against the style of the early 17th century? If used in a broader context, Wölfflin's two terms may still be applicable. There can be little doubt that the break between the static space of the middle of the century and the axial organization of, say, the 1580s roughly corresponds to the break between Wölfflin's "Renaissance" and his "Baroque." But it seems equally obvious that the line of development was not as straight as he thought. Within the sixteenth century there were cross- and counter-currents, reversals, and what may be called renewed revivals for which Wölfflin's terms are no longer adequate. Moreover, there was no sudden break; major structures like the Gesù and the Redentore offer a remarkably subtle synthesis of "conservative" and "progressive," older and newer principles of spatial composition.

Would it then be advisable to coin a new term, classicism, for the style of the 1550s and 1560s? Can the same term be applied to Michelangelo's late oeuvre, Palladio's Palazzo Chiericati, Vignola's Caprarola, and Ammannati's Pitti courtyard? To give such a meaning to the term would be to confine it in a straitjacket. It seems more promising, at least at the present time, to analyze specific trends; to characterize decades rather than a century; to recognize that some of these trends conflict or overlap with other equally characteristic currents. In this way we may also arrive at a better understanding of the work of the major architects. Building on the past and shaping the future, they transcend stylistic boundaries which are valid only for the lesser personalities.

Postscript

For a thorough discussion of the literature on Mannerism in architecture and on the periodization of Italian architecture of the Cinquecento, see Eugenio Battisti, "Proposte per una storia del concetto di manierismo in architettura," in *Odeo Olimpico 7* (1968–1969): pp. 19ff.

71. Vigevano, Piazza, looking east
(photo: van Rossum)

72. Vigevano, Piazza, looking west
(photo: van Rossum)

73. Vigevano, Piazza, southwest corner
(photo: van Rossum)

74. Vigevano, Piazza, passage to Via del
Popolo (photo: van Rossum)

75. Vigevano, Piazza, passage at the
northwest corner (photo: van Rossum)

76. Vigevano, Piazza, passage at the
northwest corner, remains of the
original decoration; after Colombo

77. Vigevano, Piazza, capitals of the
north arcades; *left,* the "new" capital
of the passage (photo: van Rossum)

78. Vigevano, Piazza, passage at the
northwest corner, exterior (photo: van
Rossum)

79. Vigevano, Piazza, south side with the Cathedral and Castle Tower (1846) (photo: van Rossum)

80. Vigevano, Piazza, capital of one of the south arcades (photo: van Rossum)

81. Venice, Library of San Marco
(photo: Venice, Böhm)

82. Venice, Palazzo Cornaro (photo:
Anderson)

83. Giuliano da Sangallo, project for
San Lorenzo; Florence, Uffizi A 278
(photo: Brogi)

165

84. Loreto, Chiesa della Santa Casa, exterior of the Santa Casa (photo: Alinari)

85. Francesco Guardi, *San Geminiano* (destroyed), detail of painting; Museo Nazionale, Palermo (photo: Brogi)

86. Andrea Palladio after Jacopo
Sansovino, project for Santa Maria
della Misericordia, Venice; Museo
Civico, Vicenza (photo: from R. Pane,
Andrea Palladio)

168

87. Venice, Loggietta (photo: Alinari)

88. Antonio da Sangallo the Younger, project for San Giovanni dei Fiorentini, Rome; Florence, Uffizi A 1292 (photo: Florence, Gab. Fot. Naz.)

89. Rome, Palazzo Farnese, Courtyard (photo: Alinari)

90. Antonio da Sangallo the Younger, project for the courtyard of the Palazzo Farnese, Rome; Florence, Uffizi A 627 (photo: J. S. Ackerman)

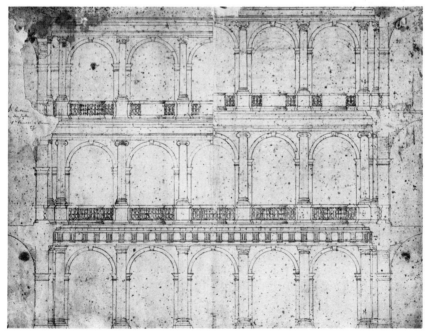

91. Montepulciano, Santa Maria presso
San Biagio, interior (photo: Alinari)

92. Ponte Casale, Villa Garzoni, facade
(photo: Fiorentini)

93. Venice, Library of San Marco, detail of Ionic order and frieze (photo: Alinari)

94. Rome, Villa Farnesina, detail of upper order and frieze (photo: Archivio Fot. Vat.)

95. Michele Sanmicheli, Palazzo
Bevilacqua, Verona (photo: Fiorentini)

96. Michele Sanmicheli, Palazzo Pompei,
Verona (photo: Fiorentini)

97. Cristoforo Lombardo, project for
Santa Maria presso San Celso, Milan
(photo: London, Victoria and Albert
Museum)

98. Vignola, project for Palazzo Bocchi,
Bologna

99. Bartolommeo Ammannati, Courtyard of the Palazzo Pitti, Florence
(photo: Anderson)

100. Galeazzo Alessi, Santa Maria di
Carignano, Genoa (photo: Alinari)

101. Galasso Alghisi, Santa Maria delle
Vergini, near Macerata, ground plan

102. Galasso Alghisi, Santa Maria delle
Vergini, near Macerata, section; Milan,
Castello Sforzesco, Biblioteca Trivulzio,
Cod. 179 (photo: Lotz)

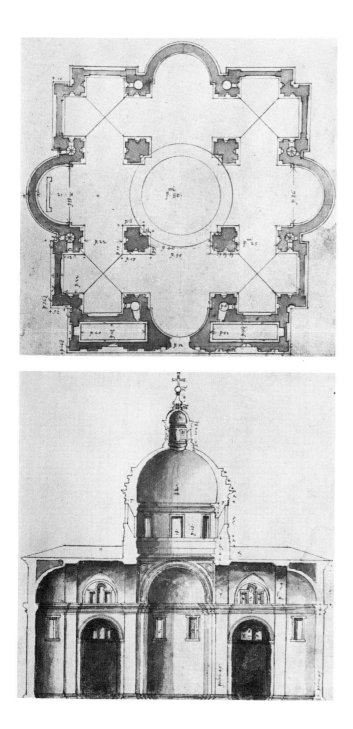

177

103. Michelangelo's project for St. Peter's, fresco, about 1585 (photo: Gab. Fot. Vat.)

104. Michelangelo's project for St. Peter's, fresco, after 1586 (photo: Gab. Fot. Vat.)

105. Vignola, Il Gesù, Rome

106. Pellegrino Tibaldi, San Fedele, Milan

107. Tribolo, Villa Castello, near Florence (photo: Florence, Gab. Fot. Naz.)

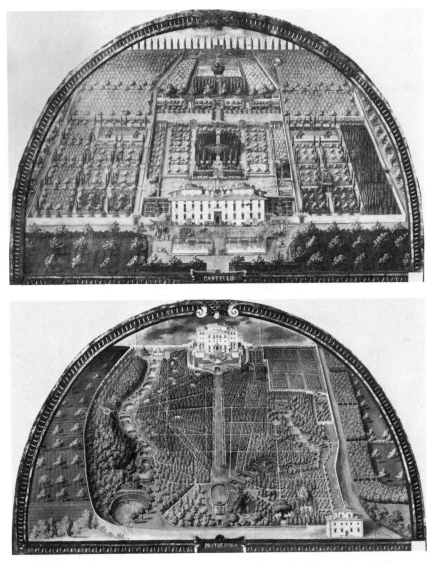

108. Bernardo Buontalenti, Villa Pratolino, near Florence (photo: Florence, Gab. Fot. Naz.)

7

THREE ESSAYS ON PALLADIO

Observations on Palladio's Drawings

Giangiorgio Zorzi's edition of the drawings of Andrea Palladio offers new insight into his artistic personality. Zorzi expresses the hope "that a . . . free and calm discussion will provide material for both the historical and the artistic study of the Master from Vicenza." It is in this spirit that I should like to discuss some questions posed by the drawings Palladio made or owned.

Interest in drawings has greatly increased ever since the Second World War. At international auctions drawings fetch very high prices, often comparable to those paid for important paintings. Drawings are appreciated as spontaneous manifestations of creativity, expressed with immediacy and unfettered by the slow process that leads to the final version of the work. There is, however, an important category of Renaissance architectural drawings that were by no means created spontaneously.

Among the drawings published by Zorzi, there is a sheet showing renderings of the Theater of Marcellus. Zorzi maintains that the drawing itself is by Falconetto and that it has annotations in his handwriting.[1] On the *verso* of the sheet, on the lower right, there is a Doric capital from the Theater of Marcellus, shown in section and in perspective (Fig. 109). The same capital, rendered in a very similar manner, appears on a page of the Codex Coner (Fig. 110), which has been thoroughly discussed in Chapter 1.[2] Two other pages of the Codex Coner show the moldings of the Theater, which appear on the left side of Falconetto's drawing: the *cimasa del menbreto ionico,* the articulation of the second-story arcade (Fig. 111), while the corresponding *cimasa del menbreto dorico* is shown reversed (folio 116).

An Ionic capital is shown on the upper left section of Falconetto's drawing. The same capital appears in the *Quattro Libri* of Sebastiano Serlio, published in 1537 (Fig. 112).[3] In addition to the frontal view, Serlio

Published as "Osservazioni intorno ai disegni Palladiani," *Bollettino del centro internazionale di studi di architettura 'Andrea Palladio'* 4(1962): pp. 61–68 gives a section of the capital, and this section, too, appears on the Falconetto sheet, although reversed. The detail visible in the right center of the sheet agrees with another illustration—again reversed—from Serlio's treatise.[4] The *recto* of Falconetto's sheet shows, on the left, the Ionic cornice of the Theater, and on the right, part of the trabeation of the Doric order (Fig. 113). The Ionic cornice corresponds accurately to the Coner drawing (Fig. 114). If the Falconetto drawing were not the reverse of the one in the Codex Coner, it might be taken for an exact copy. The same detail, however, also appears in Serlio,[5] where it faces the same direction as on the Falconetto sheet, although in Serlio's woodcut it is more roughly reproduced.[6]

The draftsman of the Codex Coner used the *braccio fiorentino* as the unit of measurement. The Falconetto drawing bears on the *recto* a note that Zorzi believes to be by Palladio: "Note that this plan [the plan of a bay of the Theater] is done with the measure here indicated and each of these measures equals a *brazio.*"[7] Zorzi has shown that Palladio normally used the *piede Vicentino* in his drawings and that on those occasions when he annotated the drawings of Veronese artists, he almost always observed that they are measured in *piede veronese* or in the *pertica veronese*. Thus, on Falconetto's drawing there is a second note which Zorzi attributes to Palladio: "This molding is drawn using the *mesura di ventura* (Ventura's measurements?), although it was measured in *palmi,* but I have converted it to the *brazio fiorentino.*"[8] A third annotation refers to the measurements of the dentils, which are represented "according to the one which Messer Michele has drawn" ["the one" seems to refer to "sheet"].[9] Thus, the seven details of entablatures shown on Falconetto's sheet are all reproduced almost identically either in the Codex Coner or by Serlio; the unit of measurement used by the draftsman was the *braccio fiorentino;* and the notes by Palladio show that the draftsman had at least two other drawings in hand, one of which was measured in *palmi.*

These observations all seem to indicate the same thing—that the "Falconetto" sheet is not an original rendering of the building, but the copy of one or, more probably, of several sources. Palladio owned the sheet and added new measurements, perhaps after checking the building itself. He also used other renderings, one of which was the work of the draftsman who had measured in *palmi,* while others may have been autographs. It is interesting that Palladio even indicates who the authors of some of these sheets were: a certain Ventura who took measurements and "Messer

Michele," who, as Zorzi maintains, may have been Sanmicheli.

It is known from numerous other examples that the procedure reconstructed here for Falconetto's drawings was the rule rather than the exception for architectural drawings of the sixteenth century, particularly in the
case of drawings made after ancient buildings. The Codex Coner, for example, is generally regarded as a collection of copies of originals going
back to the circle of Bramante;[10] and Serlio seems to refer to the same
practice. In his preface to the *Libro Quarto* (from which our examples
have been drawn) he writes: "for everything that you will find in this
book, give praise not to me, but rather to my teacher, Baldassar Petruccio
da Siena." As another example of such copying, it is worth mentioning the
sketchbook at Lille, attributed to Giovan Battista and Aristotele da
Sangallo, which also contains copies of lost originals. Indeed, the notebook
belonging to the Sienese architect Oreste Vannocci Biringucci in the
Biblioteca Comunale of Siena shows that this type of copying was still
current in the late sixteenth century. Biringucci died in 1585, shortly after
becoming architect to the Duke of Mantua. In addition to copies of
Vignola, his notebook contains a great deal of material that had already
been copied in the Lille sketchbook, drawn between 1530 and 1540.[11]

Zorzi demonstrates that a drawing by Raphael after the antique was in
Palladio's collection.[12] This observation is not without importance, for it
would appear that the sheets of Messer Michele and Ventura were not only
used by Palladio but actually remained in his possession. It has not yet
been possible to identify these two drawings, since the legacy of Palladio
has not been preserved intact.

This legacy included, I believe, a volume of architectural drawings that
passed in the late nineteenth century from the Destailleur Collection in
Paris to Leningrad, where it is no longer traceable. This volume,
Destailleur Codex B, was attributed by H. von Geymüller, with little
justification, to Fra Giocondo.[13] It dates from the second quarter of the
Cinquecento and shows structures as well as architectural fantasies. As the
handwriting and the style of drawings, such as the "Fonte Dicesi in
Borgogna," prove, the contents of the volume are not related to the work
of Palladio (Fig. 115). Yet on the last page of the Codex there is a note:
"This book belonged to Andrea Palladio."[14] I see no reason to doubt the
correctness of this inscription, which dates to the late sixteenth or early
seventeenth century. Therefore it can be established that Palladio's
collection of drawings was larger than would appear from the group that

has survived. The drawings he owned must have been essential for his antiquarian activities and for his work as illustrator of Vitruvius.[15]

Palladio turned again to older representations when he drew the Colosseum on a sheet in London (Fig. 116). The sheet, which is undoubtedly autographic, combines swift sketches with precise renderings of architectural moldings. In the center of the drawing there is a detail of the Doric order of the Colosseum, shown in section and in perspective. Here again we are dealing with a copy from the Codex Coner. The detail selected for rendering and the perspective chosen by Palladio accord so well with the corresponding details in the Codex that the connection is clear (Fig. 117). Here, however, Palladio substituted the *piede vicentino* for the *braccio fiorentino* of the Codex Coner. Furthermore, the two section drawings of the Colosseum on the *verso* of the London sheet, which are by Palladio, also go back to older models (Fig. 118). Although these sections do not correspond literally to the relevant Coner drawings on folio 39 *recto* and *verso,* the relationship is too evident to be put down to coincidence. Palladio's representation of the stairs of the lower two stories and of the profile of the facade recalls the *verso* of Coner 39 (Fig. 119), but his rendering of the corridors on the upper stories and of the rows of seats is somewhat different. These variations can be explained, however, by the section of the Colosseum given in Serlio,[16] where one finds the upper stories that are missing in the Codex Coner. Consequently, it is tempting to think that Palladio had in hand the volume of Serlio or the model that Serlio himself used. The Palladio drawing would seem to represent, therefore, a synthesis of three different older drawings—a rather complicated procedure, but one which nevertheless is understandable if we consider the difficulties and expenses involved in carrying out new renderings and measurements *in situ.*

Palladio went repeatedly to Rome, but only for a few months at a time. So it is unlikely that he drew and measured anew all the ancient buildings he represented. For that matter an analogous procedure is still to be found in twentieth-century publications. The plans and sections of the *Quattro Libri* or of Bertotti-Scamozzi are used to illustrate buildings of Palladio that are still standing.

I have only alluded briefly to the method of projection used by Palladio. As I have tried to show, the type of perspectival representation of architecture used in the Codex Coner is characteristic of architectural drawing during the first decades of the sixteenth century.[17] This kind of perspective is regularly found in drawings both from Bramante's circle and by Giuliano da Sangallo.

A new phenomenon appears in architectural drawings about 1520: orthogonal projection. The first literary mention as well as a precise description of this method are to be found in the famous memorandum of Raphael addressed to Leo X, dealing with the ancient buildings of Rome. The first drawings to use the new method are those of Antonio da Sangallo the Younger, who worked at St. Peter's under Raphael's direction from 1516. On the other hand, other contemporary artists such as Baldassare Peruzzi held to perspective representation, or to a combination of orthogonal and perspective projection.

The illustrations of the trabeation of the Basilica Aemilia in the Roman Forum, which appear in the Codex Coner and in Serlio's book, serve to clarify the difference between the two methods (Figs. 120 and 121). The Codex Coner reproduces the frieze in perspective seen slightly from below, while Serlio renders it in orthogonal projection, adding the details beneath the cornice in perspective on the right side of the page. Here once again Serlio shows himself to be the successor of Peruzzi. A similar mixture of both methods of projection also appears in some of Palladio's drawings. Thus, in his rendering of the Colosseum (Fig. 118) some details of moldings are given in perspective, while the corridors and staircases are rendered in orthogonal projection.

In the illustrations of the *Quattro Libri* Palladio always used orthogonal projection. The advantages and disadvantages of the two methods emerge with striking clarity when we compare the Doric trabeation— evidently taken from the Basilica Aemilia—in the first of the *Quattro Libri* (Fig. 122) with the corresponding drawing in the Codex Coner (Fig. 120). As Palladio's illustration shows, orthogonal projection renders details without foreshortening. On the other hand, the Coner drawing makes clear that perspective representation inevitably "distorts" dimensions and proportional relationships through foreshortening. Some more distant forms are necessarily masked by those parts that project, a disadvantage avoided in orthogonal projection, where all the moldings and every detail appear to be "complete." The perspective drawing, however, brings out the volume of the trabeation and renders the three-dimensional form more clearly, while the orthogonal projection is a more radical abstraction. Perhaps it was precisely this abstract quality of orthogonal projections that led Palladio as well to copy perspectival views. However, these views naturally had to be redrawn when they were used for the illustrations of the *Quattro Libri*.

The Palladian drawing which pairs the section of the Pantheon with the plan and section of the Temple of Venus and Roma provides a good example of orthogonal projection (Fig. 123). Zori rightly believes it to be an authentic drawing by Palladio. However, he attributes the perspective section of the same temple (Fig. 124) to Falconetto, on the grounds that when the buildings "are shown in perspective we may be sure we are not dealing with drawings by Palladio himself."[18] Evidently, the method of projection is the most important criterion for Zori when deciding whether a drawing should be attributed to Palladio rather than to Falconetto. If a sheet like the perspective of the Temple of Venus and Roma bears the handwriting of Palladio, Zorzi believes such notes to be additions.

I would prefer to believe that Palladio was less inflexible in his choice of methods of representation. We have seen him copy details from older perspective renderings. It seems equally clear that he collected them as well. The drawings by Falconetto which, as Zorzi shows, came into Palladio's possession, make a case in point. With this in mind it is but a short step to the suggestion that Palladio himself also actually drew or copied perspective renderings like that of the Temple of Venus and Roma. Surely, the master must have tried to compile the most complete and representative documentation possible both for his studies and for his publications. For these purposes the question of whether a building was shown in orthogonal projection or in perspective would have been altogether irrelevant.

The perspective view of the Temple of Venus and Roma serves precisely to show how much more clearly spatial configurations can be rendered in perspective. If we assume (although it is not fully demonstrable) that Palladio used drawings both in orthogonal projection and perspective section for the illustration of the temple in the *Quattro Libri* (Fig. 125), we would also be able to explain a striking detail in the drawing of the section (Fig. 123), namely that the coffering of the barrel vault is not shown. It is easy to show in perspective because of its plasticity, but it is far less legible when rendered schematically in orthogonal projection.

If we are right, the corresponding illustrations of the *Quattro Libri* also would have been developed from drawings done both in orthogonal projection and in perspective. I fully appreciate that this is no more than a hypothesis requiring further study—one of the many put forward.

Reflections on Palladio as Town Planner

The documents concerning Palladio's basilica in Vicenza give no indication that the architect ever thought about an overall arrangement of the buildings ringing the Piazza dei Signori and the Piazza delle Erbe (Fig. 126). In his masterly transformation of the old Palazzo della Ragione, Palladio took into account inherent structural and functional demands. Conceived as an independent monument, by its stately bulk the building dominates its surroundings, but neither the height of its loggias nor its horizontal articulation is in harmony with the earlier buildings around the basilica.

While the basilica was being built, the great transformations of the main piazzas of Venice, Rome, and Bologna were being planned and to some extent executed. The lack of integration of the basilica at Vicenza with its neighbors seems to be not the result of external circumstances, but is rather due to some precise architectural intention on Palladio's part. The building, which is conceived as autonomous, imposes its own esthetic norms on the environment and therefore does not need to be integrated with it.

A very different attitude was revealed by Giulio Romano in 1534, when he was called to Vicenza to give his opinion on the restoration of the old Palazzo della Ragione. Having put forward his suggestions for solving static and functional problems, Giulio added that "there may be no harm in submitting this memorandum so that in the course of time all the forementioned things may be done, or better, that those to come who wish to decorate and bring to completion the construction of the palazzo should lower the main piazza and raise the Piazza delle Frutte to the same level; so that all the piazzas round about will be even; and so that the palazzo may stand in the middle of a piazza, which in turn should be, at least insofar as possible, surrounded by porticoes as in a cloister."[19] His ideas correspond closely to Sangallo's slightly earlier plans for the piazza at Loreto,[20] and "the porticoes as in a cloister" suggested for the piazza at Vicenza certainly are numbered among the most interesting examples of sixteenth-century urban planning.

We can deduce from the *modus procedendi* of the Consiglio dei Cento, which decided to carry out Palladio's project for the basilica in 1549, that Giulio's proposals were known to Palladio. It is clear, however, that Palladio never considered such an integrated arrangement for the piazza.

Published as "Riflessioni sul tema Palladio urbanista," *Bollettino del centro internazionale di studi di architettura 'Andrea Palladio'* 8 (1966): pp. 123–127

For that matter, it seems that Palladio was neither consulted nor involved in any way, when a new wing was added in 1561 to the Monte di Pietà, which stands across the piazza from the basilica; this despite the fact that the new wing, the long facade of which faced the main square, was to form an integral part of the surroundings of the basilica.[21]

The decision of the Consiglio dei Deputati in 1565, taken with the construction of the Loggia del Capitanio in view, was that certain shops and houses should be purchased "to build there, as shall seem good to the city, another most beautiful loggia, which would be a work of great honor and most welcome to this whole city."[22] This decision was taken several years before Palladio began work on the loggia; and it is unlikely that he had made a design long before building activity started. The loggia was constructed because of the state of the existing fifteenth-century structure, which threatened collapse.[23] Here again the documents do not allow us to interpret the new loggia as a proposal or plan intended by the architect as a response to considerations of city-planning. Furthermore, the architecture of the Loggia Bernarda is anything but integrated with the surrounding buildings. Its colossal order is no less dominant over the piazza than the superimposed orders of the basilica opposite.

The facades of San Giorgio Maggiore and of the Redentore in Venice do not form part of the urban environment in the sense discussed here. On the other hand, the facade of San Petronio at Bologna, for which Palladio submitted several projects, faces on the main square of the city. It may be that the transformation of the other sides of the piazza—certainly under-way and perhaps even finished in 1572—led the deputies of San Petronio to invite Palladio to Bologna to prepare designs for the facade. Palladio had surely seen the Bolognese piazza when he went to Rome, so it is reasonable to assume that he realized the significance of his facade projects for the urban context.

Subsequent events confirm what has been suggested about Palladio's attitudes. In his first letter to the church administrators, dated 17 July 1572, Palladio recommended that a plan "in the German [i.e. Gothic] manner" should be adopted, because "many buildings of this kind are to be seen, and among them the finest in Italy."[24] When he gives as examples the cathedrals of Milan, Siena, Florence, and Orvieto, he is speaking of structures that dominate their respective urban environments without being integrated with the adjacent buildings in a unified piazza scheme. This interpretation of the architect's ideas is further confirmed by the fact that Palladio's drawings for the facade of San Petronio provide alternatively for three superimposed orders and a single colossal one; schemes which incidentally do not correspond to any other building on the piazza.[25]

The deliberations about the facade were protracted. In 1578 the idea was put forward to "build a portico in front of the church." Commenting unfavorably on the proposal, Camillo Bolognini, the Bolognese envoy to Rome, wrote that "either we want to consider the Church of San Petronio as a building in its own right, or else as part of the place in which it stands." Weighing the advantages and drawbacks of these alternatives, he asks "whether the addition of the portico is meant to increase its beauty and convenience [that is, of the church] or that of its site, which is the piazza."[26] The Bolognese were convinced, however, that theirs would be "the most beautiful portico in Europe and would therefore lend great majesty, not only to the Church of San Petronio and to the piazza, but indeed to the whole city."[27]

Palladio was less enthusiastic. Summoning the authority of Vitruvius, he writes that "it is quite true that the majority [of ancient temples] were built with porticoes . . . although it seems that in our times the portico is not much used." Palladio seems to betray his reluctance when he says "I could almost allow myself to be persuaded to praise the opinion of those who desire the said portico."[28]

In his next letter, which accompanied the plan commissioned for the portico, Palladio shows that he was reconciled to the idea, whether out of convenience or from conviction one does not know: "The portico—no longer built in our times—would be a most beautiful thing, and would be of the greatest convenience."[29] While Palladio gave a great deal of thought to the structural conditions imposed by the portico, as well as to the correct proportions of the orders to be used, none of his letters refers to the significance of the portico in relation to the piazza, a point clearly considered to be essential both by the church administrators and by the Bolognese envoy to Rome. In fact, the latter, referring to his first letter, explains that he had "taken into consideration the place where the portico was to be built, from which I concluded that this was likely to bring greater loss to the piazza than gain to the church . . . which was the most important point of all."[30] Although Bolognini did not doubt that "Signor Palladio would do it extremely well," he added, with a trace of bitterness, that "while one expects the rules of the ancients to be observed, this should not lead to dimming the elegance and obstructing the spaciousness of the piazza."[31]

Would it be wrong to interpret this as a subtle attack on Palladio?

Perhaps Bolognini had hoped to be supported by Palladio and was disappointed when he read that temples had porticoes "not only in front, but indeed all around and Vitruvius took great pains over this, teaching their proportions."[32]

Palladio's letters do not mention the "spaciousness and elegance of the piazza." Like the Loggia Bernarda, the facade of San Petronio was for Palladio "a building in its own right" and not "a part of the place in which it stands." The observation of the rules of the ancients—that is, the regularity and beauty of the monument itself—took priority over criteria of city-planning. The indifference to these criteria seems to be confirmed, and not, as M. Zocca thinks, denied,[33] if one reads in the *Quattro Libri* that churches should be situated "on beautiful and ornate piazzas, from which many streets lead out, so that every part of the temple may be seen in all its dignity," and so that "the facades of the temples shall be disposed in such a way that they look over the greater part of the city."[34]

The Rotonda: A Secular Building with a Dome

Palladio's *Quattro Libri* illustrate and describe more than twenty villas, only two of which have domes: the Villa Rotonda and the unexecuted Villa Trissino at Meledo (Figs. 127–128). The plans of both buildings are of the same type—a large circular hall inscribed in a square, four facades with porticoes, and the terrace from which the building rises, reached by a flight of stairs leading up to each facade. This is a type of plan resembling that of fifteenth- and sixteenth-century central churches, and, like buildings of this type, the two villas by Palladio also carry domes. Why did Palladio use this plan only for these two villas, and why is no other villa of his crowned by a dome?

The text of the *Quattro Libri* provides a partial answer to these questions. Speaking of the setting of the Villa Trissino, Palladio says: "The site is extremely beautiful, since it is on a hill surrounded by a very broad plain. On the top of the hill there is to be a circular hall surrounded by smaller rooms . . . ."[35] Of the Rotonda, he writes: "The site is as agreeable and pleasant as one could hope to find, for it is on a softly sloping hill, which is easy to climb and is surrounded by other most agreeable hills that give the appearance of a vast theater . . . , and because there are beautiful views to be enjoyed, loggias have been made

Published as "La Rotonda: edificio civile con cupola," *Bollettino del centro internazionale di studi di architettura 'Andrea Palladio'* 4 (1962), pp. 69–73 on all four sides."[36] Palladio stresses that the Rotonda, like the Villa Trissino, is on the top of a hill and is therefore visible from all sides. It is no accident that the setting of the Rotonda is compared with an amphitheater, in the center of which the villa stands. Only in such a setting is it appropriate—again in the words of the *Quattro Libri*—to build "loggias . . . on all four sides";[37] only in these two villas "on the top of the hill will there be a circular hall."[38] One notes, however, with some surprise, that Palladio makes no reference to the domes of the two buildings. To the eye of the modern visitor, however, the dome is a logical and intergral part of the architecture and essential to it. Seen from the inside, the dome forms the vault of the great hall and as such it is analogous to the vaults of churches: a circular hall demands a round vault. At the same time the dome is an essential element of the exterior of the building. Its height can be varied at will. The higher the cupola, the more monumental is the effect of the building. One need only think of the difference between the cathedrals of Florence and Siena, or between the Pantheon and St. Peter's; the dome of the Pantheon is of little importance for the panorama of Rome, although it has the same diameter as that of St. Peter's. But this is not the place to discuss the development that culminated in Michelangelo's dome; neither is it necessary to demonstrate that domes of the Byzantine type, like those of San Marco in Venice or of Sant' Antonio in Padua, give a completely different effect, picturesque rather than monumental, since they are grouped together in a fantastic cluster that crowns the structures beneath.

The Tempietto of San Pietro in Montorio gives the simplest possible demonstration of the function of the dome in a Renaissance, centrally planned building. While the domes of analogous ancient temples, like the Temple of Vesta at Tivoli or the peripteros of the Foro Boario, are barely visible from the outside, that of the Tempietto dominates the exterior precisely because it is raised on a drum and therefore is completely visible.

In the same way, the dome determines and dominates the exterior of the many churches built on a central plan in the first half of the sixteenth century. For the most part they are situated outside the walls so as to be visible from all sides, while those built inside the city, such as the Steccata in Parma, are situated on sizable piazzas. In both cases, the sites can be compared with the setting described by Palladio for the Rotonda as "in a vast theater."

Evidently, the choice of a centralized building with a dome was determined by the sites of the two villas. These sites were analogous to those chosen for centralized churches. The analogy becomes even more striking if we recall that most Renaissance churches on a central plan were built *ex novo*. They arose not out of a need to provide space for liturgical functions, but out of a desire to erect monuments in honor of sacred images of the Madonna. This interpretation is supported by the very names of these sanctuaries: La Madonna di Campagna at Piacenza and at Verona, and so on. The domes of these buildings make them into monumental tabernacles over the miraculous images.

At the same time, however, these domes go back to certain eschatological aspects inherent in the dome since antiquity. The late Karl Lehmann pointed out that the dome has always been the image and symbol of the vault—or sail—of the heavens. Indeed, in Italian the words *heaven* (*cielo*) and *sail* (*vela*) are also used as synonyms for *vault*. The eschatological interpretation of the dome was by no means forgotten in the Renaissance, as the frescoes in the dome of the Florentine cathedral show. There Vasari and Zuccari painted the Last Judgment, while God the Father appears in the "heaven" of the Chigi chapel in Santa Maria del Popolo.

Beginning in the fifteenth century, the new and purely formal value assigned to the exterior of the dome was superimposed on the older eschatological interpretation of the interior. This new function of the exterior, which could be called esthetic, arose from a new concept of the church as monument. By crowning the centrally planned villa with a dome, Palladio transferred the concept of the building as a monument from sacred to secular architecture. The Rotonda could be defined as a secular version of the type of centralized church found at Todi or Montepulciano. Furthermore, the use of the dome for a villa also reveals a new concept of the villa itself, which now becomes a monument in the sense I have already defined the term. Palladio's description of the Rotonda is unambiguous. The four porticoes, the square plan, the four flights of stairs, the site—all these characteristics are what make the Rotonda a freestanding monument and, like the churches, this monument requires a dome.

One need hardly point out that no previous villa combines all these elements. The Medici villa at Poggio a Caiano has only one facade, which is reached by means of two flights of steps, and only this facade has a pedimented portico. The Neapolitan villa of Poggio Reale, now destroyed, had an interior courtyard. The exterior was probably very simple, more like a medieval *castello* than a sixteenth-century villa. Neither can the Rontonda be compared with villas derived from the Villa Madama in Rome, such as the Villa Imperiale at Pesaro and the Genoese villa of Andrea Doria, nor with the Villa dei Vescovi at Luvigliano. None of these villas are set on the summits of hills; since they face the valley, they need only one facade. The facade can be reached from the valley by stairs that lead up from one level to the next, ending in front of the facade. None of these villas are, like the Rotonda, visible from all sides.

Clearly—and I am not the first to make this point—Palladio introduced an entirely new type into the category of buildings we call villas. It now seems possible to sum up those elements that characterize this Palladian innovation. With the Rotonda the villa is interpreted as a freestanding monument, visible from all sides; it adopts the domed monumental sanctuary type in a secular building; even the choice of a hilltop as an appropriate site represents an innovation when compared with the settings of earlier villas.

This interpretation is only partially corroborated by the text of the *Quattro Libri.* Palladio says nothing about domes. He even fails to mention them in the brief chapter of the first book, "Delle Maniere delle Volte." The dome of the Tempietto is illustrated but not described in the relevant passage of the treatise. And it is hardly surprising that the description of the Rotonda, as indeed of villas in general, should be so short and concise. Palladio speaks as an architect, not as an art historian. He is talking about facts, not ideas.

Although Palladio's writings fail to provide full confirmation of my interpretation, this does gain support from the evidence of his drawings. Among the sketches published by Zorzi, there are reconstructions of a building of the type of the sanctuary of Fortuna at Palestrina. It is a structure of vast dimensions and remarkable complexity, typical of the Hellenistic period, and synthesizing sacred and secular elements. Two versions of Palladio's reconstruction survive. While the lower part of the complex and the terraces are more or less the same, the building, which rises on the crest of the hill, is shown differently in the two versions. In the first the temple resembles the Pantheon in type: a round building with a shallow dome (Fig. 129). In the second version the structure is almost identical with the Rotonda (Fig. 130): four flights of stairs leading to four porticoes and—in Palladio's words—"on the top of the hill there is to be the circular hall"; naturally, in this case not "surrounded by smaller rooms," since the building is a temple. The difference between the two versions shows that the site did not offer any visible basis for the reconstruction. Unhampered by the evidence of remains, Palladio here could invent *ex novo*.

It is not surprising that these buildings, which were to be erected in settings so similar to that of the Rotonda, on top of a hill and apparently in the middle of a great natural amphitheater, should have been conceived on a centralized plan. If Palladio designed buildings for this site in the style both of the Pantheon and of the Rotonda, it must have been because he saw the same quality in both—both met the requirements of the site. It seems to me that this quality can be defined. Throughout the Middle Ages and until the nineteenth century, the Pantheon was the monumental building, indeed the monument *par excellence*. By substituting the plan of the Rotonda for that of the Pantheon in his second version, Palladio recognized that the type of the Rotonda also had the characteristics of a monument. Of course, the crowning dome is an indispensable element of both versions of Palladio's design.

The fame of the Rotonda was spread perhaps more widely by the illustrations of the villa in the *Quattro Libri* than through direct knowledge of the building itself. Thanks to the growing fame of Palladio's treatise and to the two buildings by Scamozzi inspired by the Rotonda, the secular building with a centralized plan and vaulted with a dome became extremely well-known throughout Europe. About 1800 Thomas Jefferson, an expert architect and student of Palladio, submitted a design for the president's house in Washington in the style of the Rotonda and, indeed, copied it rather closely. This shows that more than two centuries later the model created by Palladio in the Rotonda was still considered a form suitable to express the dignity and ambition of the head of the new nation. Once again the dome was an indispensable element of the new structure. Let us add that the new nation and its President were the first to conceive of the State as an entity entirely separate from the Church. It was, however, Palladio who freed the dome from its exclusively religious associations and made it available for secular architecture.

Notes

1. Zorzi, *Disegni,* pp. 91ff.

2. Ashby, "Drawings," p. 66.

3. Republished in *Regole Generali di Architettura* (Venice, 1566) Book IV, fol. 160 *verso.*

4. *Ibid.,* fol. 162 *recto,* the second profile from the left.

5. *Ibid.,* fol. 162 *recto,* on the far left.

6. The cornice of the Doric order,

shown on the upper right of Falconetto's sheet, appears slightly modified and again reversed *ibid.,* fol. 142 *recto.*

7. Zorzi, *Disegni,* p. 92.

8. *Ibid.*

9. ". . . . secondo quella ch'a disegnata messer Michele" (*ibid.*).

10. For the authorship and the dating of the Coner drawings and the *modus misurandi* of their draftsman, see also B. Lowry, Review of J. Ackerman, *The Cortile del Belvedere: The Art Bulletin* 39 (1957): pp. 163ff.

11. For the relationship between the notebooks at Lille and Siena, see Ackerman, *Michelangelo* 2: Catalogue 1.

12. Zorzi, *Disegni,* Figs. 264–65, and p. 105.

13. Geymüller, "Trois Albums de dessins de Fra Giocondo," *Mélanges d'archéologie et d'histoire d'art, Ecole francaise de Rome* 11 (1891): pp. 133ff. (hereafter "Trois Albums"); see also the additions by Lanciani, *ibid.,* pp. 159ff., as well as the comment by C. Huelsen, *Römische Mitteilungen* 7 (1892): p. 274, for the attribution of the drawings. Photographs of the Codex are in the German Archeological Institute, Rome.

14. The note on the provenance of the Codex is on fol. 130 *verso,* as has been noted in Geymüller, "Trois Albums," p. 138.

15. Other architects of the sixteenth century are no less interesting in this respect than Palladio. This is still true of seventeenth- and eighteenth-century architects. Professor Heinrich Thelen, who is preparing the catalogue of Borromini's drawings, was kind enough

to tell me that Borromini owned a very large number of drawings by old masters. In the early eighteenth century the Swedish architect, Nicodemus Tessin the Younger, acquired several thousand architectural drawings, which are now in the National Museum in Stockholm.

16. Serlio, *Regole Generali di Architettura* 3: fol. 79 *verso* and 80 *recto.*

17. See Chap. 1.

18. ". . . sono resi prospetticamente si puo essere sicuri trattarsi di disegni non del Palladio" (Zorzi, *Disegni,* p. 33).

19. The letter was first published by Antonio Magrini, *Memorie,* app. p. 32; see also Giangiorgio Zorzi, *Contributi alla Storia dell' Arte Vicentina sui Sec. XV e XVI* 3 (1937): p. 146.

20. Uffizi A 922; cf. G. Giovannoni, *Sangallo,* 1: 194; 2: Fig. 140; see also idem, *Saggi,* pp. 285ff.

21. For the Monte di Pietà cf. F. Barbieri, R. Cevese, and L. Magagnato, *Guida di Vicenza,* 2d ed. (Vicenza, 1956), pp. 95ff.

22. Magrini, *Memorie,* p. 168, and app., p. 62.

23. According to Magrini, *ibid.,* pp. 162–163, there stood on the same site an older structure which had "the form of a loggia . . ." and for which there is evidence in the Vicenza archives from 1410 on.

24. Magrini, *ibid.,* app., pp. 25–26.

25. See the discussion of Palladio's designs for the facade of S. Petronio by W. Timofiewitsch, "Fassadenentwürfe Andrea Palladios für S. Petronio in Bologna," *Arte Veneta,* 16 (1962): pp. 82ff.

26. Letter of 10 December 1578 to the

Confaloniere di Giustizia in Bologna (G. Gaye, *Carteggio* 3: p. 410).

27. Statement of Camillo Paleotto of 20 December 1578, addressed to the *Operai* of S. Petronio; (Gaye, *Carteggio* 3: p. 413).

28. Letter to Giovanni Pepoli, dated 12 January 1579 (Gaye, *Carteggio* 3: p. 417; and Magrini, *Memorie,* app., p. 62; Palladio had "veduto e considerato il parere del Sig. Bolognino e le sue bellissime raggioni, e medisimamente la sua buona risposta del signor Palleotto" (*ibid.,* p. 61).

29. Letter of 27 January 1579 to Giovanni Pepoli (Gaye, *Carteggio* 3: p. 418; and Magrini, *Memorie,* app., p. 63).

30. Letter of Camillo Bolognini to Giovanni Pepoli, 20 February 1579 (Gaye, *Carteggio* 3: pp. 420ff.).

31. *Ibid.,* p. 421.

32. See note 29.

33. "Le concezioni urbanistiche di Palladio," *Palladio,* n. s., 10 (1960): pp. 69ff.

34. Palladio, *Quattro Libri* 4: p. 1.

35. *Ibid.* 2: p. 60.

36. *Ibid.:* p. 18.

37. *Ibid.*

38. *Ibid.:* p. 60.

Postscript to Observations on Palladio's Drawings

The complex problem of the attribution of the drawings from Palladio's estate, which are now in the R. I. B. A. collection in London and in the Museo Civico at Vicenza, has been thoroughly and convincingly discussed by Howard Burns in *Palladio. Catalogo della Mostra* (Vicenza, 1973), pp.133–154. For the Codex Coner see now Tilmann Buddensieg, "Bernardo della Volpaia und Giovanni Francesco da Sangallo. Der Autor des Codex Coner und seine Stellung im Sangallo-Kreis," *Römisches Jahrbuch für Kungstgeschichte* 15 (1975): pp. 89ff.

Postscript to Reflections on Palladio as Town Planner

This essay should be read in conjunction with James S. Ackerman's publication of "Palladio's Lost Portico Project for San Petronio in Bologna" in *Essays in the History of Architecture Presented to Rudolf Wittkower* (London, 1967), pp. 110ff. For Antonio da Sangallo's projects for the piazza of Loreto, mentioned in note 20, see now Kathleen Weil-Garris Posner, "Alcuni progetti per piazze e facciate di Bramante e di Antonio da Sangallo a Loreto," in *Studi Bramanteschi: Atti del congresso internazionale,* 1970, Milan, Urbino, Roma (Rome, 1974), pp. 313ff.

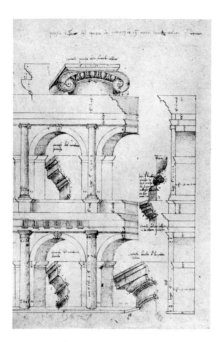

109. G. M. Falconetto (?), Rome,
Theater of Marcellus; London,
R. I. B. A. X: 20 *verso* (photo: Rome
Gab. Fot. Naz.)

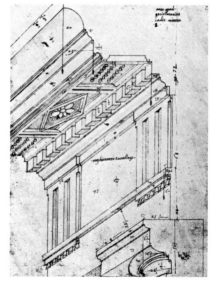

110. Rome, Theater of Marcellus, Codex
Coner fol. 76 *recto;* London, Sir John
Soane Museum (photo: Bibliotheca
Hertziana)

111. Rome, Theater of Marcellus, Codex
Coner fol. 115 *verso;* London, Sir John
Soane Museum (photo: London,
Courtauld Institute)

112. Ionic capital from Theater of
Marcellus; from Serlio, 1566 ed., IV,
fol. 160 *verso*

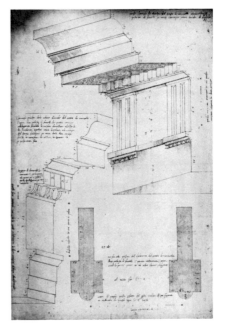

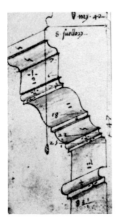

113. G. M. Falconetto (?), Rome,
Theater of Marcellus; London,
R. I. B. A. X: 20 *recto* (photo: Rome,
Gab. Fot. Naz.)

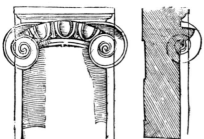

114. Rome, Theater of Marcellus, Codex Coner fol. 93 *recto;* London, Sir John Soane Museum (photo: London, Courtauld Institute)

115. Anonymous, "Fonte dicesi in Borgogna"; Destailleur Codex B fol. 130 *recto* and *verso*, formerly Leningrad, Hermitage (photo: Bibliotheca Hertziana)

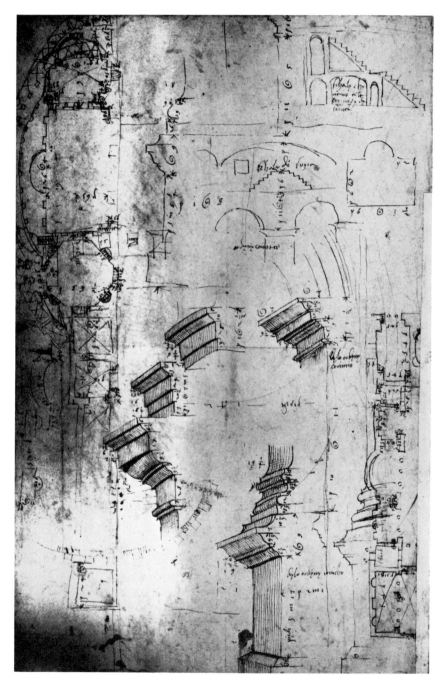

116. Andrea Palladio, Rome, Colosseum
and Baths of Caracalla; London,
R. I. B. A. VIII: 14 *verso* (photo: Rome,
Gab. Fot. Naz.)

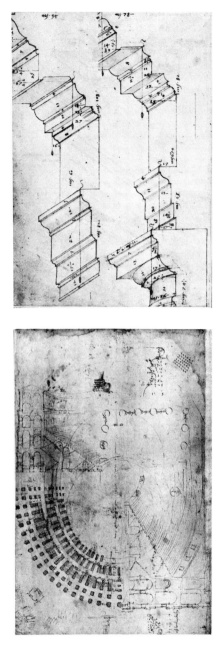

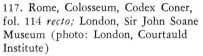

117. Rome, Colosseum, Codex Coner, fol. 114 *recto;* London, Sir John Soane Museum (photo: London, Courtauld Institute)

118. Andrea Palladio, Rome, Colosseum; London, R. I. B. A. VIII: 14 *recto* (photo: Rome, Gab. Fot. Naz.)

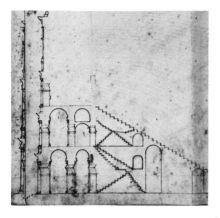

119. Rome, Colosseum, Codex Coner, fol. 39 *verso;* London, Sir John Soane Museum (photo: Rome, Gab. Fot. Naz.)

120. Rome, Basilica Aemilia, Codex Coner, fol. 61 *recto;* London, Sir John Soane Museum (photo: London, Courtauld Institute)

121. Sebastiano Serlio, "Dell'Ordine
Dorico," from 1566 ed., 4: fol. 142
recto

122. Andrea Palladio, "Dell' Ordine
Dorico," from *Quattro Libri* I: 27

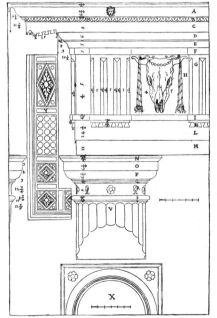

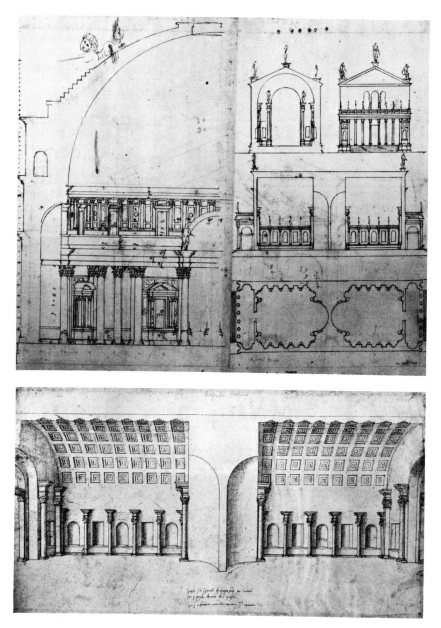

123. Andrea Palladio (?), Pantheon,
Rome, Temple of Venus and Roma;
London, R. I. B. A. VIII: 9 verso
(photo: Rome, Gab. Fot. Naz.)

124. G. M. Falconetto (?), Rome,
Temple of Venus and Roma; London,
R. I. B. A. IX: 25 (photo: Rome, Gab.
Fot. Naz.)

125. Andrea Palladio, Rome, Temple of
Venus and Roma; *Quattro Libri* IV: 38

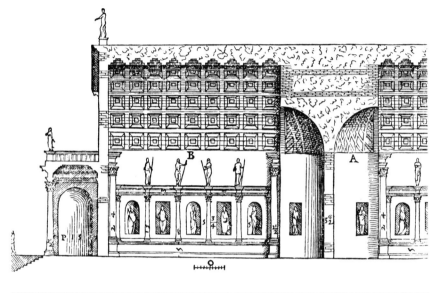

126. Vicenza, Piazza dei Signori (photo:
Vicenza, Chiovato)

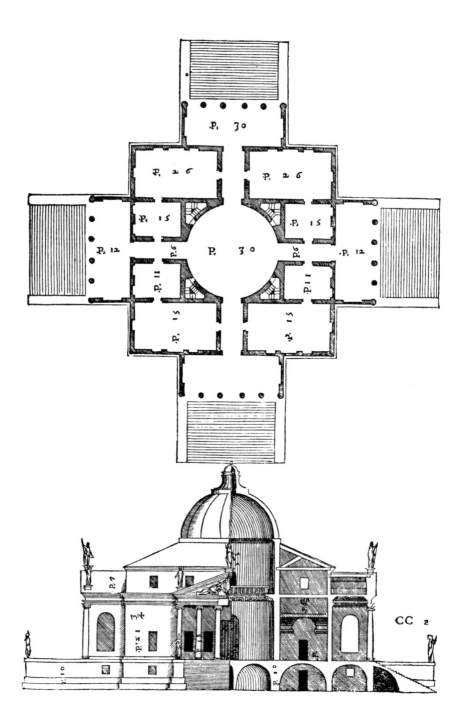

127. Andrea Palladio, Vicenza, Villa Rotonda

128. Andrea Palladio, Villa Trissino at Meledo (from *Quattro Libri* II: 19; ground plan and elevation from *Quattro Libri* II: 60)

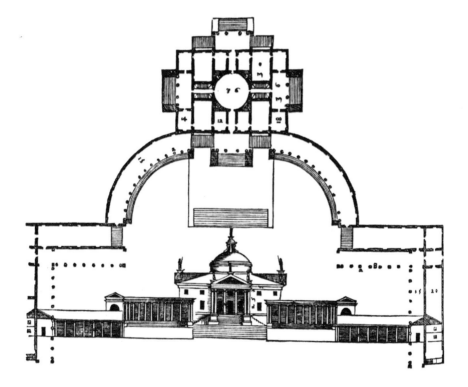

129. Andrea Palladio, Reconstruction of the Sanctuary of Fortuna at Palestrina; London, R. I. B. A. IX: 5 (photo: London, Courtauld Institute)

130. Andrea Palladio, Reconstruction of the Sanctuary of Fortuna at Palestrina; London, R. I. B. A. IX: 7 (photo: London, Courtauld Institute)

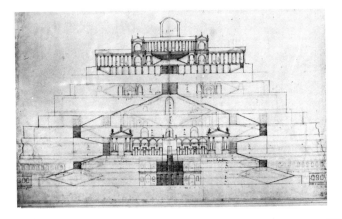

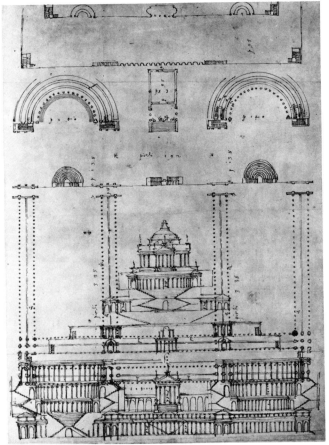

SELECTED
BIBLIOGRAPHY

Ackerman, James S. "Architectural Practice in the Italian Renaissance." *Journal of the Society of Architectural Historians* XIII, 3 (1954): pp. 3–11.

————. *The Architecture of Michelangelo,* 2 vols. London, 1961.

————. "The Belvedere as a Classical Villa." *Journal of the Warburg and Courtauld Institutes* 14 (1951): pp. 70–91.

————. *The Cortile del Belvedere.* Vatican City, 1954.

Alberti, Leon Battista. *Dell' Architettura, Libri Dieci.* Translated by C. Bartoli. Milan, 1833.

————. *Della Pittura e della Statua.* Milan, 1804. (For *Della Pittura* also Ed. L. Malle, Florence, 1950).

————. *De re aedificatoria* (Latin Text and Italian Translation). G. Orlandi, ed. Milan, 1966.

Ashby, Thomas. "Sixteenth Century Drawings of Roman Buildings, attributed to Andreas Coner." *Papers of the British School at Rome* 2 (1904): pp. 1–88; 6 (1908): pp. 184ff.

Barbaro, Daniele. *De architectura libri decem* (Italian Translation: *I dieci libri dell'architettura di M. Vitruvio*). Venice, 1556–67.

Barucci, Galileo. *Il Castello di Vigevano.* Turin, 1909.

Berghoef. "Les Origines de la Place ducale de Vigevano." *Palladio,* n. s. 5, 14 (1964): pp. 165–78.

Biffignandi, Pietro Giorgio. *Memorie*

Storiche della Città e Contado di Vigevano, 2 vols. Vigevano, 1870.

Boito, Camillo. *Il Duomo di Milano.* Milan, 1889.

Bruschi, Arnaldo. *Bramante Architetto.* Bari, 1969.

Burckhardt, Jakob. *Der Cicerone.* Basel, 1855 (Reprinted in vols. 3, 4, *Gesamtausgabe,* 14 vols. Stuttgart, 1929–34).

Cattaneo, Pietro, *I Quattro primi libri di architettura.* Venice, 1554.

Colombo, Antonio. "Armi e leggende sulla facciata della Piazza Ducale, detta del Duomo di Vigevano." *Archivio Storico Lombardo* 4, no. 15 (1911): pp. 180–88.

————. "La Piazza Ducale, detta del Duomo, in Vigevano, e i suoi restauri." *L'Arte* 5 (1902): pp. 248–52.

————. "Vigevano e la Republica Ambrosiana nella lotta contro Francesco Sforza (Agosto 1447—Giugno 1449)," *Bollettino della Società Pavese di Storia Patria* 2 (1902): pp. 315–377; 3 (1903): pp. 3–38.

Coolidge, John. "The Villa Giulia: A Study of Central Italian Architecture in the Mid-Sixteenth Century." *The Art Bulletin* 25 (1943): pp. 177–225.

De Bernardi Ferrero, Daria. "Il Conte Ivan Caramuel di Lobkowitz, Vescovo di Vigevano, architetto e teorico dell'architettura." *Palladio* n. s. 15 (1965): pp. 91–110.

Degenhart, Bernhard. "Dante, Leonardo und Sangallo." *Römisches Jahr-*

buch für Kunstgeschichte 7 (1955):
pp. 101–292.

De Rossi, Giovanni Giacomo. *Insignium Romae templorum prospectus.* Rome, 1683.

Egger, Hermann. *Codex Escurialensis.* Vienna, 1906.

Fabriczy, Cornelius von. *Die Hand-zeichnungen des Giuliano da Sangallo.* Stuttgart, 1902.

Filarete. *Treatise on Architecture.* Edited by J. R. Spencer. 2 vols. New Haven, 1965.

Frankl, Paul. *Entwicklungsphasen der neueren Baukunst.* Leipzig and Berlin, 1914.

Frey, Dagobert. *Bramantes St. Peter-Entwurf und seine Apokryphen.* Bramantestudien, vol. 1. Vienna, 1915.

Gaye, Giovanni. *Carteggio inedito d'Artisti.* 3 vols. Florence, 1839–40.

Geymüller, Heinrich von. *Les Projets primitifs pour la Basilique de Saint-Pierre de Rome.* Paris, 1875.

Giovannoni, Gustavo. *Antonio da Sangallo il Giovane.* 2 vols. Rome, 1959.

———. *Saggi sull'architettura del Rinascimento.* 2d ed. Milan, 1935.

Golzio, Vincenzo. *Raffaello nei documenti, nelle testimonianze dei contemporanei e nella letteratura del suo secolo.* Vatican City, 1936.

Heydenreich, Ludwig H. *Leonardo da Vinci.* Basel, 1953.

Huelsen, Christian. *Il Libro di G. da Sangallo. Codice vat. lat. Barb. 4424.* Turin, 1910.

Huntley, G. H. *Andrea Sansovino.* Cambridge, Mass., 1935.

Kauffmann, Hans. "Über 'rinascere', 'Rinascita' und einige Stilmerkmale der

Quattrocentobaukunst." *Concordia Decennalis.* Cologne, 1943, pp. 123–46.

Kent, William Winthrop. *The Life and Works of Baldassare Peruzzi of Siena.* New York, 1925.

Kletzl, Otto. *Planfragmente aus der deutschen Dombauhütte von Prag in Stuttgart und Ulm.* Stuttgart, 1939.

Lotz, Wolfgang. "Entwürfe Sangallos und Peruzzis für S. Giacomo in Augusta in Rom." *Mitteilungen des Kunsthistorischen Instituts in Florenz* 5 (1937–40): pp. 441–44.

Lotz, Wolfgang. *Vignola-Studien.* Würzburg, 1939.

Magrini, Antonio. *Memorie intorno la vita e le opere di A. Palladio.* Vicenza, 1845.

Malaguzzi Valeri, Francesco. *La Corte di Lodovico il Moro.* 2 vols. Milan, 1913–15.

Manetti, Antonio. *The Life of Brunelleschi by Antonio di Tuccio Manetti.* Edited by H. Saalman. University Park, Penna. & London, 1970.

———. *Vita di Filippo di Ser Brunellesco.* Edited by E. Toesca. Florence, 1927.

Marchini, Giuseppe. *Giuliano da Sangallo.* Florence, 1942.

Nava, Antonia. "Sui disegni architettonici per S. Giovanni dei Fiorentini." *Critica d'Arte* 1 (1935/36): pp. 102–8.

Oertel, Robert. "Wandmalerei und Zeichnung in Italien." *Mitteilungen des Kunsthistorischen Instituts in Florenz* 5 (1937–40): pp. 217–313.

Paatz, Walter and Elisabeth. *Die Kirchen von Florenz.* 6 vols. Frankfurt-am-Main, 1952–55.

Palladio, Andrea. *I Quattro libri dell'architettura.* Venice, 1570.

Papini, Roberto. *Francesco di Giorgio Architetto.* 3 vols. Florence, 1946.

Pastor, Ludwig von. *History of the Popes from the Close of the Middle Ages.* Edited by R. F. Kerr. 40 vols. London, 1891–1952.

Pevsner, Nikolaus. *Outline of European Architecture.* 6th ed. Harmondsworth, 1960.

Plan und Bauwerk. Exhibition Catalogue, Munich, 1952.

Ramella, Vittorio R. "Il Castello Sforzesco di Vigevano." *Castellum* 7 (1968): pp. 69–74.

Redtenbacher, Rudolf. *Mitteilungen aus der Sammlung architektonischer Handzeichnungen in der Gallerie der Uffizien zu Florenz, I: Baldassare Peruzzi und seine Werke.* Karlsruhe, 1875.

Sacchetti, Egidio. *Vigevano Illustrato.* Milan, 1638.

Serlio, Sebastiano. *Tutta l'opera d'architettura et prospettiva di Sebastiano Serlio* (including *Regole Generali di Architettura*). Venice, 1619. Reprint Ridgewood, N.J., 1964.

Solmi, Edmondo. *Scritti Vinciani.* Florence, 1924.

Thieme, Ulrich and Becker, Felix. *Allgemeines Lexikon der bildenden Künstler von der Antike bis zur Gegenwart.* 37 vols. Leipzig, 1907–50.

Vasari, Giorgio. *Le opere di G. Vasari.* Edited by G. Milanesi. 9 vols. Florence, 1878–85.

Venturi, Adolfo. *Storia dell'arte italiana.* 11 vols. Milan, 1901–40.

Vitruvius. *Ten Books on Architecture.* Translated by M. H. Morgan. Cambridge, Mass., 1914.

Willich, Hans. *Jacopo Barozzi da Vignola.* Strassburg, 1906.

Wittkower, Rudolf. *Architectural Principles in the Age of Humanism.* 3d. ed. London, 1962.

————. "Michelangelo's Biblioteca Laurenziana." *The Art Bulletin* 16 (1934): pp. 123–218.

Wölfflin, Heinrich. *Renaissance and Baroque.* Translated by K. Simon. London, 1964.

Zorzi, Giangiorgio. *I Disegni delle antichità di Andrea Palladio.* Venice, 1959.

INDEX